19 Masks People Wear

How to See Beyond the Masks;
Exploring Emotions and Identity
as a Path to Self-Discovery,
Strengthening Communication and
Inner Fulfillment

Brian Basterfield

© Copyright Brian Basterfield 2023 - All rights reserved.

The content contained within this book may not be reproduced, duplicated or transmitted without direct written permission from the author or the publisher.

Under no circumstances will any blame or legal responsibility be held against the publisher, or author, for any damages, reparation, or monetary loss due to the information contained within this book, either directly or indirectly.

Legal Notice:

This book is copyright protected. It is only for personal use. You cannot amend, distribute, sell, use, quote or paraphrase any part, or the content within this book, without the consent of the author or publisher.

Disclaimer Notice:

Please note the information contained within this document is for educational and entertainment purposes only. All effort has been executed to present accurate, up to date, reliable, complete information. No warranties of any kind are declared or implied. Readers acknowledge that the author is not engaged in the rendering of legal, financial, medical or professional advice. The content within this book has been derived from various sources. Please consult a licensed professional before attempting any techniques outlined in this book.

By reading this document, the reader agrees that under no circumstances is the author responsible for any losses, direct or indirect, that are incurred as a result of the use of the information contained within this document, including, but not limited to, errors, omissions, or inaccuracies.

Contents

Introduction   1

1. The Power of Masks   7
   Exploring Human Behavior and Identity
       The Essence of Masks: Unmasking Human Behavior
       Unveiling the Sociological and Psychological Aspects of Wearing Masks
       The Psychology of Masking: Unraveling the Inner Dynamics

2. Unveiling Motivations   45
   Understanding Why People Wear Masks
       Exploring Motivations Rooted in Insecurity and Societal Expectations
       The Psychological Drivers of a Masked Identity
       Past Trauma and Individual Experiences: Shaping Your Masked Identity

3. Types of Masks   65
   Revealing the Different Facades People Adopt
       1. The "Pleaser"

    2. The "Perfectionist"
    3. The "Comedian"
    4. The "Intellectual Expert"
    5. The "Rebel"
    6. The "Caregiver"
    7. The "Adventurer"
    8. The "Victim"
    9. The "Protector"
    10. The "Chameleon"
    11. The "Optimist"
    12. The "Admirable"
    13. The "Nonchalant"
    14. The "Competitor"
    15. The "Martyr"
    16. The "Free Spirit"
    17. The "Influencer"
    18. The "Seductress"
    19. The "Loner"

4. Seeing Beyond the Masks   97
   Techniques for Uncovering Authenticity
     The Art of Discernment: Recognizing Authenticity
     Empathy and Active Listening: Connecting on a Deeper Level
     Developing Intuitive Insights and Cultivating Emotional Intelligence
     Unmasking Yourself: The Journey of Self-Awareness

5. Building Genuine Connections — 125
   Nurturing Meaningful Relationships in a Masked World
   - Embracing Authenticity: The Foundation of Genuine Connections
   - The Power of Effective Communication: Fostering Trust and Openness
   - The Role of Vulnerability and Emotional Intimacy
   - The Challenges of Vulnerability and Emotional Intimacy
   - The Rewards of Vulnerability and Emotional Intimacy
   - Cultivating Empathy, Compassion, and Respect

Conclusion — 151

References — 161

A Free Gift to The Readers

Thank you for choosing to read this book. I hope you find it insightful and practical.

To enhance your experience and provide additional value, I've included the following material at no extra cost to you:

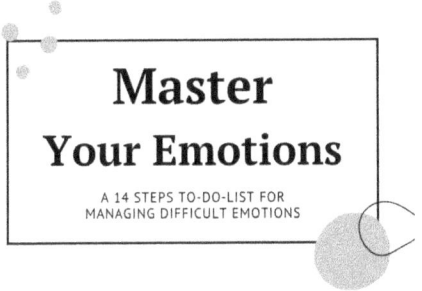

This supplementary content offers valuable insights related to managing your emotions.

To access your bonus material, please scan the QR code below:

Thank you for your support, and enjoy your reading!

Introduction

Behind every mask there is a face and behind that, a story. —Marty Rubin

Human connection as we know it, stands the test of time. If only you knew that you've been carrying a mask for most of your life. If only you knew that the people you speak to every single day were doing the same. What would you do if you knew what mask you had on today? Would you have the courage to take it off and trust? Or would you keep it on for who knows how long because it made you feel safe?

I get it—our safety is important. But what about authenticity? The desire for human connection where the masks we hold no longer disguise who we truly are inside?

There were times as a child when we craved human connection. We loved the tenderness from our parents when we got hurt or felt sad. We found solace in their touch and empathy. We felt proud when we did a good job at school, and we'd be commemorated for our efforts by our peers and our teachers. But throughout these years, that connection began to dwindle, and before we even realized it, we started carrying a mask. Or masks, depending on how you looked at your experiences.

Obviously, not a physical mask but an invisible one that felt like our security blanket. It began to hide who we truly are from the world in fear that we don't mess the connection up. Somewhere along the way, our self-expression and individuality became obsolete and rather than use our authenticity to attract remarkable beings into our lives, we began to seek external validation and conform to society's own view of who we are. Rather than focusing on what we think and believe about ourselves, we allowed society to dictate our individuality and therefore, we felt misunderstood and unheard.

Perhaps we experienced bullying, and that journey was enough to disguise our true selves and put on the masks that became a part of our life. Or perhaps our parents were too busy to spend time with us so we did whatever we could to seek their affection, love, and care by trying to be the perfect child. We craved that human connection, the desire to form real and authentic relationships with the people in our life, but somehow it got replaced with misunderstanding and the misuse of our voice.

I understand that you may be struggling to form genuine connections right now. Perhaps you've been hurt multiple times and you're unsure of who to trust. Maybe you feel misunderstood, and you don't know how to express yourself in a way that people listen and understand where you're coming from. You struggle to accept yourself and allow others to accept you with the fear that "you're too much" or "not enough." This has made you lonely, isolated and wondering if your life will ever change.

Here's what I want you to know: It's okay to mask who you are for a time. You're getting to know yourself, the right connections to build and who brings great value into your life, even for a season. By using your masks—yes, sometimes there are multiples—you're able to weed out the people who don't really fit into your life because they don't bring value or appreciate who you truly are, inside and out. They don't allow you to express your individuality in a way that is right for you, not for society. They want you to be who you're not, just so you can be liked and gain their trust.

Currently, you may feel disconnected to the world and perhaps even question your self-connection, but don't worry—a few tweaks in the right direction and your journey will start to make sense. I understand that the world may be a bit complex, but that doesn't mean your authenticity and genuine connection with others has to be. You have the power to change your story and you have the power to let go of your masks with the right individuals who encourage you to do so. The important thing to remember is to take your time and build the trust and integrity you require within yourself and others so the relationships you build are deep, profound, and incredibly abundant.

In this book, you'll gain the following:

How to gain a deeper understanding of human behavior and the many masks that people wear.

How to connect with others in a way that creates an unbreakable bond.

How to build more meaningful relationships where you create a circle of trust, opportunity and understanding.

How to improve your self-awareness and understand the masks that you hold and why they're a part of your life in the first place.

How to build a deeper relationship with yourself in a way that unveils your authentic self with love and acceptance.

How to overcome any trust issues that are holding you back from fostering genuine connections with others.

How to create an authentic life worth living that is empowering, regardless of living in a masked world beyond your control.

Believe me—I've been there. I have met many people from all walks of life and there was a time when I struggled to trust... *anyone*, not even my own shadow. Every time I stepped outside my front door, I put on a mask. A mask that would disguise my self-expression and uniqueness. I'd like to believe that I brought a ton of value to the people I met, but there were pieces of my journey where I felt that I couldn't trust anyone who appreciated this value, authenticity, and creativity. Because of this, I preferred to hide it from them, and the masks went on. Until, of course, I was ready to take them off. They stayed on until I truly believed I could trust the people that I was with to value my authenticity without judgment and misunderstanding.

Could this be you? Since you're reading this book, perhaps. Think of this book as an enlightenment, a path toward genuine human connection. A path that leads you to understand your own authenticity and helps you understand that of the people around you. It may not be easy to trust, especially with the journey you're going through, but know this: it is not impossible. Just as it can be easy to meet people and form sounding relationships, it can be just as easy to foster that connection and understand and appreciate each other on a deeper, more profound level.

You owe it to your authenticity to be heard, loved, and respected for all your worth. The first step is to understand how your masks play a role in your life and the impact they have on your identity, self-expression, and acceptance. Thank you for going on this journey and shining a light on authentic connection, self-empowerment, and a deeper sense of value. Here's to creating the most powerful relationships you will ever encounter moving forward.

Chapter 1

The Power of Masks

Exploring Human Behavior and Identity

To begin this chapter, we must recognize the power masks hold in our lives.

There is no doubt that the masks we wear possess an undeniable allure—a captivating mystique that piques our curiosity and beckons us to uncover the secrets they hold. I don't know if you've ever had the pleasure of attending a masquerade ball, but if not, visualize the scene with me for a moment.

The allure of the ballroom, the mystery of the evening, and the sophistication of the ambiance. Everyone is dressed to the nines, and you are surrounded by an array of ornate masks that conceal the faces of each guest, including yourself. So many beautiful masks befall you, and you can't help but wonder what the story is behind each glance. Each mask represents a unique story, a hidden aspect of someone's being, and the transformative power of disguise.

But, beyond that, the invisible masks that we wear, the ones that are attached to our personality, carry profound weight. They symbolize the traits we're afraid of showing to the world around us. The fear can migrate through our entire being and be strong enough to use our masks and conceal our true identity. We try to be someone we're not in order to be liked, loved, appreciated, and acknowledged. They shape societal human behavior in such a way that, at times, we are unable to tell the difference between realism and fallacy.

This chapter is about going beyond the theatrical concept of masks. Rather than step into a masquerade ball, we're stepping into how the psychological component permeates our life in simple yet profound ways that become life-changing. If we're not aware, it can permanently become our reality.

We'll discuss the following facets of mask wearing including:

- The concept of masks and their significance in human behavior. We must understand how greatly they can affect our lives and how they can influence our association with others.

- The profound impact mask wearing has on shaping our sense of self and the way we allow others to view us.

- The reasoning of why we wear masks in order to adopt a different persona and identity. I believe this is more than just wanting to be liked.

At the core, masks serve as our vehicles for self-expression and identity. If we fear how others would react to our authentic self, we put them on, not because we truly want to, but simply because we feel we need to protect ourselves. Our masks allow us to choose the parts of us that we want others to see while keeping other parts hidden and free from potential judgment and criticism.

We carefully choose the masks we wear to shape how we are perceived by others. For example, being the life of the party may not be our true self, but to protect our shyness, we wear the mask of confidence. We may be sad and depressed, but yet, we use our smile as our mask at social gatherings and the like. If we're experiencing struggling times, such as scarcity, we wear the mask of faith and happiness so no one can tell we're merely surviving and treading above water. All of these masks provide us with a safety net, a tool so to speak that we can leverage however way we wish, especially if we feel that it's the only thing we can control.

There is so much more I can say about this, but it's best to dive deeper into the content so you understand what all of this means. As we continue to explore the power of masks in this chapter, I invite you to witness the transformative effects they have on us as well as society while also acknowledging the delicate balance between authenticity and performance. By gaining a deeper understanding of the profound significance of masks in shaping human behavior and identity, it will help you identify how they currently shape your life and what you can do to rectify it.

The Essence of Masks: Unmasking Human Behavior

So many of us may not realize the incredible power that wearing metaphorical masks might have on our lives and the ability to connect with the people around us. Wearing a mask, especially with certain people, can affect how we make an imprint in their lives. For a time, putting on our masks can help us get to know others and reveal our full identity when we're ready. If we don't feel comfortable, the mask goes on and we can choose when to take it off and how long we leave it on for. This can greatly affect a few things in our behavior:

- Whether we can release our boundaries and allow others to get a taste of our authentic nature.

- The way we feel challenged to step out of our comfort zone and allow others, even if just met them, to see exactly who we are.

- The way we choose to create a completely new identity in front of certain people in fear of them not liking our authentic selves.

- Whether we are comfortable enough to release

the layers that we are portraying in order to divinely connect with others.

For example, let's say you're attending your first networking event. You have just launched your business and you are ready to meet new people and get your name out into society. However, as an introvert, you are certainly stepping outside of your comfort zone to do something new you've always had a fear of doing.

Before the event, you decided to slip on the metaphorical mask of confidence and extroversion. You choose to stand tall, and despite your shyness, you try to step into extroversion. You are launching your business and looking to meet people, so you don't want them to know that you are actually a shy and introverted individual. At the networking event, you become someone different. People may love to hang around you due to your confidence, but in reality, you are nervous, your heart is racing, and all you want to do is go home and crawl into your cave.

At the event, you put on a professional facade that makes people like you. You may feel overwhelmed and anxious, but the mask of confidence didn't allow you to feel that way. Instead, it becomes your source of empowerment and provides you with the courage you need in order to navigate a social setting, such as a networking event.

Why didn't you want the people to know the real you? It comes down to one important reason: If you lack confidence in speaking about your business and you're shy around people, how will you ever be able to meet your potential client? This is a question that becomes a bit of a double-edged sword. You may be more of an introvert rather than an extrovert, but in these situations, wearing the mask of confidence can help you achieve your goal; and of course, first impressions matter, so wearing the mask and keeping it on however long it is needed can help you reach the next-level.

This is just one example of the psychological significance of masks. When it comes to human behavior, our masks become the bridge between our inner selves and the external world. This allows us to project qualities that align with a specific situation we're facing or the desired image we wish to portray.

Depending on the situation, we may don masks of strength, humor, or bravery, even if we don't feel we are funny, strong or courageous internally. Embracing these masks allows us to constitute a sense of empathy and compassion for others as well as ourselves. When we wear our masks, we experience a sense of empowerment and self-inspiration. They allow us to explore different characteristics that we, with practice, can perhaps adapt to our unique persona. In a way, they become a repertoire of new characteristics that help us experience our behavior in a different way. They offer us a sense of control in the way that we want others to perceive us, and they empower us to navigate situations that are unfamiliar to us.

Hiding Our True Identity

When we wear our masks, an interesting phenomenon bestows upon us—the ability to conceal our true identity and behavior. Our masks become veils that shield a few concepts of our life from the outside world:

- our vulnerabilities
- our insecurities
- certain parts of ourselves that we might feel inadequate
- our ability to fear judgment, criticism, or rejection

By making these parts of us "invisible" to the naked eye, we can protect ourselves from potential hurt or shame. Instead, we can use our masks to create an altered version of ourselves that the world may like and enjoy. This helps us navigate uncomfortable social situations with ease and allows us to don a new persona that people may accept. It also allows us to expand our curiosity and embrace parts of us that we never knew existed.

However, when choosing to hide behind a metaphorical mask, such as confidence or fearlessness, it can greatly affect the way we connect and communicate with others. These masks can create a barrier between who we truly are and who we are pretending to be. If we constantly try and pretend to be someone we're not, it can create unnecessary friction with human connections and hinder genuine conversations with others. This can become a negative attribute that people grow to understand about us, and the potentiality of authentic trust and faith in us can dissipate. Instead of creating authentic and valuable connections, false misrepresentation of our personality and character can cause people to reject us and feel uneasy about having a true relationship with us.

So, by hiding our true identity and behavior with our masks, how can it affect the way we interact with others? There are a few ways:

Superficial Connections

When we wear a masked version of ourselves when interacting with others, such as at a networking event or party, we can only engage in surface-level conversations. For example, we might only discuss specific topics or do our best to avoid any conversations that require us to reveal our true thoughts, emotions, or vulnerabilities. We might also shy away from sharing our opinion in fear it may be rejected or judged. Because of this, our connections can lack authenticity or fulfillment and can feel invaluable. It can also make us feel like we don't know who our true friends are or who to lean on when we're experiencing a challenge. This can make us lose faith and trust in humanity and in finding true connections who genuinely care to build a lasting and profound relationship with us.

Not Feeling Aligned With Ourselves and Others

When we wear our masks, we might often experience misalignment between our inner selves and the person we project to others. For example, we might say certain things or agree with other's beliefs in order to be liked, but on the inside, it contradicts our own values. We might also dress a certain way, but when we look at ourselves in the mirror, it doesn't represent our true self.

Feeling misaligned with our true self can create a barrier that blocks us from achieving authentic happiness and fulfillment. It can feel inauthentic, which can cause shame within us and create a disconnection to our authenticity. By not recognizing the misalignment and becoming aware of it, we can go deeper into the rabbit hole and eventually lose our unique identity and adopt a new persona that lacks genuineness to the core of who we truly are.

Experiencing the Fear of Rejection

One of the biggest fears when desiring to express our authenticity is the fear of rejection or feeling judged and criticized. If that fear is strong prior to creating connections and meeting people, it will motivate us to put our masks on and to keep them on for as long as we feel the need to.

We may think the following:

If I avoid showing this aspect of my personality, they won't run in the other direction.

I may be too much for people, so I'll try and dial down my personality as much as I can.

What if people don't like me if I fully show who I am? It's best to keep certain parts hidden until I can trust them enough not to reject me.

All of these thoughts become the motivator you need to wear your masks. They could be the mask of confidence, fearlessness, extroversion, transformation, and the like. We choose to hide certain aspects of our identity or modify our behavior to fit societal bias and what society expects of us.

For example, if we attend an event where the attendees are more conservative, we might tone down our personality when having conversations with others. We might talk less or tone down the way we speak. We might even dress more conservatively and reformed so we can fit in with this particular crowd and not feel secretly judged because of what we're wearing. Of course, experiencing the fear of rejection can prevent us from forming genuine connections with others, and it can prevent us from expressing our unique self-expression.

Lack of Trust and Intimacy

In order to create and foster genuine relationships, we must build trust and faith in ourselves and others. This can take time, patience, commitment, and dedication.

When we choose to wear a mask, however, it can present our true character in a different light than what we expect it to be. This can feel challenging and difficult for others to trust us; they may even shy away from truly connecting with us as the relationship doesn't feel genuine or authentic.

For example, there is a well-known movie that explains what I mean in a highly effective way. As the main character is getting ready for a date, she does what she can to become the woman she feels her date will like. Authentically, she is not super intellectual, but she tries to dress the part and have conversations in a way that doesn't feel authentic to her. Instead, it feels false, but she tries to adopt this new persona anyway so that her date goes well. Instead, her date can sense the falseness and turns his back on her because he prefers to date women who are not afraid of expressing their authentic self.

This is just an example among many that demonstrates that in order for people to trust you and express interest in creating a relationship with you, you must be okay with sharing your authentic self with them.

Suppresses Our True Emotions

When we try to hide our true behavior and identity behind a mask, or many masks, it might cause us to also hide how we're feeling in the moment. If we're feeling sad, depressed, anxious, or fearful, we might push them down to our core and bury them in fear that they show our weakness rather than strength.

Based on certain levels of societal expectations and bias, these emotions can be perceived as a weakness, therefore, we prefer to stray away from allowing others to see us experience them.

For example, if we're experiencing financial struggles and treading above water, this may make us feel depressed, anxious, and sad. However, when people ask us how we're doing, rather than express vulnerability, we will generally reply with, "I'm doing amazing. Life is good. How are you doing?" This answer masks the sorrow we feel in fear that we may be judged for being vulnerable. If we feel severely depressed, we might also mask it with the mask of happiness in front of others, so they don't worry or judge us because to them, we live a great life.

By pushing down our emotions, a few things can happen:

- We lose a deep connection with ourselves.

- We struggle with having faith in ourselves and regulating our emotions.

- We create a barrier between connecting deeply to ourselves and expressing our vulnerability to others.

- We can emotionally blow up at a moment's notice. The negative emotions can appear strongly in our core, and by suppressing and ignoring them, we lose a sense of control and can explode without expecting to.

Rather than hide them, we must learn to acknowledge and accept them, so we have the opportunity to create an emotional connection with ourselves and others.

When we can understand how great of an impact hiding our true identity and behavior can be when we are interacting with others, it allows us to reflect on the many masks we wear and the consequences they can have on our relationships. To be honest, it makes us think about how much value we are truly bringing to the table by creating a different persona when we are around others. What if we chose to be ourselves? I mean, really be ourselves, vulnerability and authenticity intact. Would our relationships feel different? Would there be more trust to confide in each other?

Every time we put on our masks, we must ask ourselves these questions. We must reflect on the answers in a way that takes away our fear and lack of confidence in our own unique self-expression and identity. By learning to embrace our true selves in all our glory—fears, flaws, and all—it becomes a profound invitation for others to do the same, which in turn, fosters an extraordinary environment full of trust, empathy, and true, genuine connections. By learning to let go of our masks and allowing our unique identity to shine through, we create an opportunity for meaningful connections and empowering conversations. We are able to flourish, inspire, and empower others as we create value with our stories and the lessons we've learned throughout our journey. By embracing our vulnerabilities and allowing ourselves to be seen, we open the door to transformative relationships and a richer, more fulfilling human experience.

Unveiling the Sociological and Psychological Aspects of Wearing Masks

The Japanese say that you have three faces:

   1. The first face, you show to the world.

   2. The second face, you show to your close friends and family.

3. The third face, you never show anyone. It is the truest reflection of who you are.

As I think about this, it's an interesting reflection. Why would we have three different faces to show to certain people? Could it be because fear is instilled within us of feeling judged, criticized, or ridiculed for being authentic? Or perhaps we're close to our friends and family, so we show them a different face but yet, still keep them at a distance because of the same fear?

As I ponder on the third face, it makes me realize that this is the face that is rarely shown to anyone but ourselves. Perhaps we have that fear, or perhaps it's because we are protecting ourselves from potential hurt and shame of being truly who we are. Expressing vulnerability and the full expression of our identity could have some psychological trauma that has yet to be healed, therefore, we prefer to keep our third face to ourselves.

In any case, I felt it important to explore the sociological and psychological aspects of wearing our masks so we can understand why we wear them on a deeper level. We're diving into the multifaceted nature of masks, exploring the sociological and psychological aspects that encourage us to don our three different identities.

Within society, we may adopt a completely different identity with one group of people and then another with a different community. More often than not, our identities are not fixed, but we work in certain aspects of ourselves, based on societal norms and expectations.

For example, when you are in a serious relationship and you first meet your in-laws, you may adorn a different identity, so they don't have an opportunity to judge you; or the judgment is minimal. If your father-in-law is a lawyer, you may try to speak intellectually in order to impress him. If your mother-in-law is in the fashion industry, you might do what you can to "dress to impress." This is by human nature and what society teaches us to do and has been teaching us for ages.

Our personality or the way we behave may have the tendency to disrespect or dishonor some cultures, therefore, we will do what we can to tone our self-expression down, so we don't come off as rude or ignorant. When meeting our partner's friends for the first time, we might adopt a different personality or hide certain parts of ourselves so we can make a great first impression. No matter how much we may dislike it, society influences what mask we put on today and it shapes our behavior, our self and worldly perception as well as what we choose to believe.

In the following sections, we will explore the psychological motivations that motivate our decisions to put on our masks and the impact they can have on our self-perception and social interactions.

Masking in Society: Constructing Our Identity Based on Societal Standards

By human nature, our identity is not considered divinely orchestrated from when we are born. It is shaped, identified, and constructed by the way we are brought up in society and in the way we continue evolving.

Our identity is usually shaped by three concepts:

- societal norms
- expectations
- cultural influences

When we embrace our masks, it is because we are putting in every effort to fit in with society, even if that means acknowledging and conforming to their expectations and being influenced by specific cultural standards. Our masks allow us to navigate our place in society so we can be socially accepted, appreciated, and respected.

Although our masks have become a crucial tool to survive in a world where social acceptance is important, and it has been for years, we must understand how they are affecting us on both a sociological and psychological level.

The norms, rules, and expectations of society that have shaped our behavior, the way others view us as well as what we believe have been guiding principles for what is appropriate and acceptable. They have been psychological teachings that have constantly reminded us of what we need to do in order to be liked and accepted as a worthwhile member of society.

As you've been going through your journey, these thoughts may have crossed your mind:

I am not enough.

I am not worthy.

I have difficulty being fully accepted by others.

These thoughts, among others I'm sure, have been your guiding compass in how you are showing up in the world. More than likely, they are thoughts that have influenced the idea that your masks are required in order to fulfill what is expected of you so you can be accepted. They're thoughts that have proved your lack of social acceptance time and time again. Because they linger in your mind and drive your decisions, being fully yourself is no longer on your radar. In fact, it is almost non-existent, and you have chosen to create a new persona, an alter ego so to speak. This alter ego, or full-fledged mask, has allowed you to create a sense of belonging and be accepted by anyone you may meet. Of course, your new persona reverts back to much of your old self when you're around those you trust, such as your friends and family; or when you're at home, you can dial down your new persona and allow your authentic self to rise.

When we're adapting ourselves to society, the pressure to keep up with expectations and show face can be immensely stressful. It can feel incredibly overwhelming to conform to society's standards of who they want you to be, even though you know in the back of your mind that being the real you is best.

From what I can envision, there are three underlying fears that hide behind the masks we wear:

- fear of rejection
- fear of judgment
- fear of social exclusion

Every day, we crave the idea to be liked... by everyone. We do all that we can to be socially accepted, loved, and embraced. If society ridicules us or chooses not to accept us, or even deems us unworthy, it breaks our heart; but more so, it becomes the fuel to keep our masks on and create a new persona and hide the traits we feel are not accepted.

A great example of this is when we attended high school. You were perhaps bullied all the time, due to what you looked like, the clothes that you wore, and how you spoke or what you chose not to say. Or maybe, you did all that you could to be accepted by the "popular" crowd. You dressed differently, did your hair like theirs, and enrolled in the same activities—it became your mission to be part of this crowd. Why? Because they were always socially accepted by the school. They got good grades, they came from a wealthy family most of the time, they were usually the teacher's pet and everyone, including your own friends loved to be around them.

Now here's the thing: While everyone, including yourself, was trying to get in with the popular crowd, those kids were wearing masks of their own. Perhaps they lacked confidence, just like you. Or perhaps, they had a lot of pressure coming from their parents to do well in school and to be liked, so they donned their own masks. No one would really notice that though. Instead, the popular crowd only showed what they wanted others to see and the people around them only paid attention to their surface level personality. They wanted a piece of popularity, so they were not socially excluded or rejected at their school.

As we continue to explore the incredible impact that society has in shaping our identity and how our masks play a role in this creation, we will understand the pressure of human behavior to become what society wants us to become. By gaining an understanding, we become aware of how everyone uses their masks to navigate the complexities of social acceptance and inclusion.

The Influence of Social Norms

When influenced by social norms and expectations, we must find a common ground between expressing our authentic selves and conforming to what society deems appropriate.

It may be difficult to find a balance, especially since we have become used to adorning our masks as much as possible, but understanding what is socially acceptable and using that to work in our authenticity can be the best of both worlds. In society, there are usually specific parameters that one should follow in order to be fully accepted.

For example, there may be specific rules we need to follow based on religious and cultural beliefs or even the beliefs and characteristics of being brought up in our family. For instance, you may be brought up in a family where it is not deemed acceptable to express your emotions or embrace your femininity. Perhaps you were taught to only conform to masculinity and embrace the go-getter stereotype and suppress the idea of being vulnerable and expressing your emotions. Even though you may have a sensitive side, you are more compelled to adopt a mask of toughness and strength and push down your sensitive nature in order to avoid ridicule and judgment from your family. Because of this avoidance, you choose to wear these masks, which is also known as the mask of conformity, to fit in with your family, which in turn, sacrifices your authentic self-expression. Rather than embrace your emotional side, you put up a wall to protect yourself as a way to fit in with the familiar mold you have been brought up with.

Another example is the societal pressure that the Royal family experiences every single day to adhere to a specific standard. They have specific obligations and expectations that they are required to conform to, and if they break away from these standards, they are immediately judged and criticized. For instance, they are required to speak and behave a certain way, dress as per royal blood expectations, and act in a specific manner. There is even a specific way they are required to eat and drink, regardless of whether they are in the public's eye or at home. This is how they have been brought up since they were children. If they experience public scrutiny, they are required to put on a mask of strength and confidence so they can handle the challenges that come their way with dignity and honor.

The pressure to conform to social norms has influenced us to don many masks throughout the years. It begins as children, and as we grow up, these norms have become deeply ingrained in our subconscious mind and influences our decision-making as well as how we form our identity and sense of belonging. We learn about social pressure from a very young age, and adorning our masks has helped us overcome these challenges. We learn about ourselves through the many masks we wear, which continually reminds us that we will know when the right time will be to take off our masks and embrace our authentic identity for good.

Integrating Into Society Using Masks

When we're learning to integrate into society, we tend to put on our masks, so we feel comfortable and included. It is our way of fitting in at school, work, and sometimes with our friends and family or when we're meeting people for the first time. Wearing our masks helps us navigate a few issues we may struggle with:

- acceptance by others
- self-acceptance
- creating connections
- navigating conversations comfortably
- fitting into society and creating a sense of belonging

In a way, wearing our masks offers us some kind of solace in our own skin. There are times when we may feel a bit anxious, especially in an uncomfortable social setting, so we use our masks as a way to feel less nervous. For example, someone might make a joke that we don't understand, and while everyone is laughing, we're internally scratching our heads, therefore, we'll use our own laughter as a mask so we can fit in with the crowd and feel accepted.

Another example is when we just start a new job. We may have coworkers that go out for a drink every night, and even though we don't like drinking, we'll go so we have an opportunity to learn more about them and create relationships. We might even say things about our life that stretch the truth, but we do that so we are liked, and our transition doesn't feel as uncomfortable. We create a different persona within us that is different from who we truly are so we can make our experience enjoyable and fulfilling. It's a way to create a sense of belonging in any environment and to create strong relationships.

However, although our masks may serve a huge purpose when integrating into society and fostering long-term relationships, we must ask ourselves this: How am I being authentic? Am I showing the full scope of my uniqueness? Or is this only a temporary solution to integrate successfully? Will it make me happy in the long run? Do I fear that they will find out that this is not truly who I am down the road and perhaps cut off the relationship I worked hard to build?

These questions are important to reflect on the next time we have an opportunity to integrate into a new society. Wearing our masks might be a great strategy in the beginning as a way to gauge the genuineness of the relationship, but how long should we keep them on?

I understand that this can be a difficult question to ponder, especially if you've fully embraced your masked persona, but I encourage you to keep in mind that revealing your authentic self to others is the best thing you can do for your own well-being. Wearing your masks all the time can lead to more negative consequences than good as time goes on. You may feel like you've lost your identity and you don't know who you truly are anymore. You may create an entirely different persona that is not the true reflection of you, and deep down, you feel like you have no control over that person. You might even express internal shame and fear because you're unsure of whether your relationships will stick around if you reveal your authentic self. You might even tone down parts of your authentic self so you can feel accepted, which can make you feel guilty that you're not expressing your fullest potential. You're trading off parts of your authenticity in order to create a sense of belonging and self-worth; while that idea sounds good in your head, internally, you're battling with yourself and creating a sense of disconnection.

As you integrate into different communities and start building connections, it is important you find a balance between the masks you wear in the beginning and when you are comfortable taking them off and integrating your authentic self into the community. When you're ready to reveal your authentic self to society, you must do so with pride, knowing that you will feel fulfilled fostering strong relationships based on genuine connection rather than masked connection.

Masking in a Cultural Society

In the last two points, we've covered the aspects of using masks to hide your true identity in society so you can feel socially accepted; this point will discuss a concept about masks that is slightly different from societal bias.

In a specific culture, masking plays a significant role in shaping your identity and fostering genuine connections. As a collective society, you might use your masks to create authentic relationships with others from your culture.

For example, you might broaden your heritage and cultural traditions by using your masks to express their value and importance. You might don your traditional cultural garments at parties or festivals, and you might integrate your culture into the food you eat and activities you participate in. Your cultural masks can provide a sense of belonging within you and allow you to express your individuality and creative self-expression when participating in your community.

For example, when you're attending a highly cultural event, you might want to express how important your cultural values mean to you by wearing a traditional outfit and participating in the dances you grew up with.

In the Philippines, for instance, when a young woman turns 18 years old, her parents organize an extravagant birthday party called the *Debut*, filled with cultural traditions so they can integrate her into society and present her to potential suitors. Traditional garments, such as the *barong* for men and the *filipiniana* for women, are usually worn to express respect and value for the Filipino heritage. They are not required to wear this, however, it's a way of reinforcing the importance of the culture in the community.

As you integrate into a less traditional society, however, such as in your workplace, you may embrace a different identity. You might not wear your cultural garments but opt for more comfortable attire that helps you feel accepted at the workplace. You will speak English with your coworkers, rather than your native language that you usually speak at home. Depending on the cultural environment, you have the ability to adapt your behavior, personality, and appearance and embrace both, which allows you to express a multifaceted identity with different people. This can be used as an extraordinary opportunity to meet people from all walks of life and get to know their own appreciation and understanding of their own culture. It can help you create unique connections and make the relationship fun and exciting as you're able to learn about different cultures and how they differ from your own.

The Psychology of Masking: Unraveling the Inner Dynamics

Our actions, behavior, and identity are usually shaped by past patterns that stay in our subconscious mind. So, when we think of why we use masks from a psychological point of view, it helps us to realize and understand a few things:

- What we might be trying to hide from others.
- What parts of our identity and behavior we are ashamed of revealing.
- What makes us afraid of trusting people enough to let them into our authenticity.
- When we started using our masks in the first place.

All of these things are a part of our subconscious mind, and they stay there until we understand the root cause; when we finally understand, it will feel easier to let go of our masks and reveal our true, authentic selves.

As you go through this section, I encourage you to reflect on these questions:

- What motivates you to wear your masks?
- How do you feel when they're on?
- How do you feel when you are your most au-

thentic self?

- What are you most afraid of when revealing your authenticity?
- Do you like the person you become when you wear your masks?

Answering these questions for yourself will help you understand yourself on a psychological level. It will help you understand what emotions you go through and what thoughts are in your mind when you wear your masks versus when you take them off. These questions will also help you reflect on what your current behavior is and what you need to do to reshape the identity that is most unique and authentic to you.

Using Your Masks to Shield Vulnerabilities

So why do we truly wear our masks? Why do our masks seem to be an important piece of our everyday wear?

In my personal experience, I have used my masks as a way to protect my vulnerabilities from getting out to the wrong people—the ones who would somehow use them as opportunities to judge, criticize or ridicule me. When they were on, I felt better. My self-esteem and confidence were positive. People showed up in my life, encouraging me to allow my true self to shine. But finding these people seemed like a difficult feat in the beginning; because of this, my masks went on as a protective shield that safeguarded my vulnerabilities, flaws, and imperfections.

Psychologically speaking, on a positive note, the masks are great for getting you over the hump of uncomfortable social interactions. The interactions don't feel complex, but rather they feel easier to navigate. Our masks give us the confidence to proceed with any interaction that comes our way; they are our safety net to manage feeling insecure, fearful, or lack confidence because the people that we meet don't like our true selves.

For example, if you have just started a new job and you're extremely nervous and feel like you're going to have a panic attack, especially if you struggle with social anxiety, you will wear a mask that helps you exude confidence. Inside, you may be feeling nauseous, and your palms might be sweaty, but on the outside, you are walking with confidence and speaking to others as if you have high self-esteem. When you get home, you are free to ditch the masks and be your socially anxious self again; but at least, when you're at work, your masks help you control how others perceive you, and you can get a firm grasp on the strong, confident person that you truly are.

Let's also say, for instance, that you struggle with severe imposter syndrome. Experiencing this is a vulnerability that you prefer not to reveal to anyone, in fear they may think of you in an unflattering light; so, during meetings and presentations, you express your infinite knowledge and wisdom as a leader, mentor, and professional. In your mind, you may believe that everyone else is more knowledgeable and intelligent, but you wear a mask of confidence and authority, so your team doesn't see that side of you. But after the presentation, you're beating yourself up because you should've said something different or presented a topic in a different way. Although this second identity may be the real you, in my opinion, so is the first person—the one that exudes confidence, supreme leadership, and genuine authority. It's only when the situation presents itself, such as during the meeting, that you choose to showcase a certain identity to help you better navigate the situation.

In a way, this protective mask helps you cope and overcome difficult situations that make you uncomfortable. It helps you get through the situations with ease and in a way that doesn't test your strength too much. It is important to remember, however, that although your masks protect you from potential judgment, you must find the balance between how they protect you and when it's time to take them off so both sides of you can shine and attract genuine connections that last for a lifetime.

Using Your Masks to Role-Play and Adapt

One of the ways you can use your masks is to become a completely different person. To create a persona that may not be a true reflection of your inner self, but it is a persona that you know everyone will like and enjoy, including yourself.

Psychologically, you can use your masks as a way to role-play and adapt to certain experiences and situations. You can role-play into the person that you prefer to show to others and modify your actions and behavior to fit that mold. You can emphasize specific traits, skills, and characteristics that help you adapt to uncomfortable situations. For example, you may be a huge introvert and overly sensitive, but you step into a persona that is extremely extroverted and always has an emotional wall up. One that constantly exudes confidence, high esteem, and strength. Of course, your introverted self may find it difficult to be the life of the party and fully immerse yourself as an extrovert in social situations, but you find a way to adapt to this person successfully in order to meet people and expand your network.

When I think of role-playing, I think of watching a play or other theatrical events. The characters portray a certain character, one that might not be similar to their true selves, but they do it to help them adapt to the situation; in this case, the scene in which they're acting in.

When it comes to real-life examples, we may adapt our character, behavior, and actions to that of a good friend or coworker. We may be at a party and witness our friends authentically enjoying themselves and attracting people from all walks of life. Psychologically, we study their behavior and their demeanor, wondering how it feels so easy for them to meet people. Before we know it, we've adapted our own behavior to be similar to theirs in hopes we'll receive the same attention. In a way, we immerse ourselves in becoming exactly who we portray ourselves to be, but in our own skin and with our unique flair. Role-playing helps us adapt and be comfortable in social interactions and helps us interact in a way that is accepted and enjoyed by others.

One of the benefits of using your masks to role-play is that you're able to understand what you like and don't like about yourself. You can create different personas and pretend to be someone else for a while in order to understand your unique identity and the authentic mark you bring into the world. This can help you understand yourself on a deeper level and allows you to understand what feels authentic and what is simply not part of, and never will be your unique self-expression.

Using Your Masks for Acceptance

Among the many reasons we wear our masks, one specific one comes to mind: acceptance. When we don our masks, we usually share certain traits about ourselves that we feel are accepted by others. When we behave in a certain way, we do it because we know that other people will accept it and invite us into their circle.

These behaviors are accepted by others, and although they may not express the full truth of who we are, we adapt them into our life and hide the attributes that we feel may be "too much" for people.

For example, when we struggle with external validation, we might dress a certain way, adapt our behavior and actions to the likes of others, and perhaps speak in a way we're not used to. Although we will feel accepted, it can cause us to lose sight of who we are authentically and step into this persona for a long time, even though it might not feel aligned.

So why do we sometimes obsess with acceptance? This is because we are usually driven by the need for human connection and belonging. We crave a sense of belonging so much in various stages of our lives that we will do whatever it takes to create a circle of trust around us. This could mean that we project certain qualities of ourselves and hide the others or adapt to societal norms and expectations of how people want us to be.

For example, when you were a child, one or both of your parents wanted you to go into a specific profession as an adult. Perhaps, your father was a doctor, therefore, he wanted you to go into the medical field and become a doctor. Or maybe your mother was a lawyer and pushed you to get your law degree and set up your own practice. There may have been a time when you craved your father's affection and acceptance so strongly that you did whatever you could for his attention, even if that included going to medical school when you dreamed of becoming an artist. Your father expected you to do this, and due to external validation and the desire to belong and to feel accepted, you obliged. You projected your father's interest in your life, even though it may not feel authentic, because you craved the acceptance that you may not have received as a child.

If you're using your masks to feel a sense of belonging, it could be due to a few reasons:

- You're struggling with the fear of rejection.
- You struggle with the fear of being seen as someone others might not accept.
- Your true self hasn't helped you meet a trust circle of people you can count on; in retrospect, your authentic self somehow failed you.

But here's the thing I want you to remember. Although your masks will help you feel accepted for a time, there will come a time when they may not be enough. You might be willing to change all that you are for someone who feels like they belong, but eventually, it may feel a bit lonely because you're not sure who your true friends are. And the pressure to maintain that image every day can do more harm than good to your emotional well-being. I encourage you to create a balance between the desire for external acceptance and authentic self-expression. In my experience, I have learned that when I learn to fully accept myself and embrace my flaws, imperfections, and vulnerabilities, others will accept me just the same.

Using Your Masks for Self-Discovery

When we wear masks to conceal our true selves, we can use them as a means of self-discovery. We can use them to explore different versions of ourselves, which allows us to do a couple of things:

- Create a deeper relationship with ourselves.
- Explore the versions in a way that allows us to find different facets of ourselves that may not have been on our radar before.

Our masks help us communicate parts of us to others that may not be easy to reveal if we didn't have them on. The interesting thing about our masks is that they are invisible. They are not shown to the naked eye; they only exist in our mind. And, although that's the case, they still help us reveal the parts of our identity that we have consciously hidden because of fear or insecurities.

Psychologically speaking, our masks are a natural part of our everyday life. No one really knows we have them on, unless we let them in on our true selves. But if not, people wouldn't really know the difference—this is why it is sometimes difficult to let go of our masks because we've adopted our masked identity so strongly that, at times, we don't even know who our true self is.

Using our masks for creative self-expression also helps us become more intentional with who we are, what we do, and who we allow to be part of our authenticity. We're able to define our unique values, express our culture and heritage in a way that is unique to us, and fully immerse ourselves in how we choose to self-represent. It becomes a unique journey of self-discovery, expression, and self-preservation.

I'm sure there have been many instances in your life where you have allowed your true self to shine, and they've taken advantage of it. This journey allows you to preserve your authenticity for those who truly matter to be a part of your life for the long haul, rather than fully express your authentic self to those who may not fully appreciate it.

By going on a journey of self-discovery with your masks, you can break from societal expectations and judgment and be exactly who you are in all your glory. If you're unsure of who that is at the moment, you can use your masks to explore different facets of your identity and identify which parts align with you more than others.

Chapter 2

Unveiling Motivations
Understanding Why People Wear Masks

Every day, we don a particular type of mask. For many, many years, masks have been more than the ones we choose for masquerade galas or the face coverings we've been using during the pandemic.

When we naturally wear a metaphorical mask, such as the mask of happiness or of confidence, we must understand the ultimate reasons why we put them on in the first place. There is no doubt that these masks affect our human behavior and the way we present ourselves to the world, but learning to let them go so we can show up as our most authentic selves is the challenge.

Every day, we interact with people who don their own masks so they can interact with us and not feel uncomfortable in any given situation. I have noticed that wearing our masks is a fact of life; it has become our natural state of being in a world of societal judgment, expectations, and bias.

But why do we wear them, that's where the reasons become unique. They are authentic to us, and they have become a part of our mission and our purpose to feel accepted.

This chapter will cover a few key components of the humanistic approach:

- Identifying the root causes of why we wear our masks.

- Understanding how the roles of fear, insecurity, and societal expectations play in our lives when it comes to wearing our masks.

- Understanding the psychological factors of why we wear our masks to fulfill our desire for acceptance, protection, and control.

- Understanding how past traumas and unique life experiences can influence our need to wear our masks and shape the underlying behavior associated with them.

By covering these topics, we can peel back the layers and gain deeper insight as to why we wear our masks and why others choose to wear theirs. Perhaps we're protecting ourselves from the potential judgment that might arise if we show certain parts of ourselves. Perhaps we feel that hiding parts of ourselves is better for our mental well-being. Or perhaps we have experienced rejection or criticism multiple times, therefore, we feel it's better to create this persona as a self-infused brand ambassador, so we don't experience that form of hurt and disrespect again. There are many reasons why we wear our masks; this chapter is about uncovering them so we can start to feel an ounce of freedom toward letting them go. This chapter is also about going through a unique self-discovery journey so we can understand our motivation behind wearing our own masks as well as understand what barriers they are creating between genuine connections and our authentic selves. When we understand ourselves on a deeper level, we can remind ourselves that although we are only human, showcasing our imperfections are what makes us unique and valuable to the world.

Exploring Motivations Rooted in Insecurity and Societal Expectations

When we are about to make decisions that make us feel uncomfortable, what usually happens? Fear gets in the way—fear of rejection, judgment, or failure. Insecurity gets the best of us, and we lose confidence in that moment. And the idea of trying to please everyone and do what is expected of us makes us want to put on our masks and create a different persona a thousand times over.

When we wear our masks, there is usually a deep motivation behind it that keeps us rooted in being someone else. This motivation makes us feel like we have no other choice but to adorn our masks for as long as we can put up the charade. Most often, we might not want to wear our masks and instead allow our inner self to shine, but there comes an uncomfortable incident that makes us feel like this is the best option to feel accepted. And this is the thing about acceptance—we live in a world where most of us will stop at nothing to fit in, even if that means creating an entirely different person altogether. We might be financially struggling, but we will go to an event looking like a million bucks; no one can really tell the difference. We might have extreme social anxiety, but donning the mask of confidence helps us exude the confidence we need to overcome our nerves when speaking with others. We can be perceived one way by our friends and family and a completely different way by coworkers and people we meet for the first time.

When we experience fear because of a certain situation, people might see it as a sign of weakness, therefore, our masks help us overcome these feelings and hide them with more empowering emotions. If we crave to be liked, appreciated, and accepted, we don't want anyone to think less of us, therefore, our masks give us the motivation we need to live at peace with ourselves and others where chasing acceptance is no longer on our radar; it is already a part of our lives.

The Influence of Fear on Human Behavior

One of the greatest attributes of fear is that it has the ability to control our lives and every decision that we make. It can stop us from stepping into uncomfortable opportunities or opportunities where the results are not consciously known. If we're wearing our masks due to internal fear, it can be an extraordinary motivator and make us feel afraid of what will happen if we take them off.

There are a few fears that can motivate us to continually wear our masks and create a barrier between our authentic selves and the persona we allow others to see: fear of judgment, rejection, and vulnerability.

Fear of Judgment

Among all, I would say this is the most common fear we can experience. Fearing that we are being judged all the time can get us into a huge frenzy; we want to keep our masks on and never take them off.

For example, if we start a new job in a new town or go to a different school than what we're used to, we risk experiencing judgment from others. In the forefront of our mind, we feel like we're being judged by the clothes we wear, the type of car we drive, or the food we eat, so to mask our true feelings, we might go shopping for a new outfit or purchase different food than what we're used to. The world is full of societal norms and expectations, so to "keep up with the Joneses" as one would say, we adapt to what is expected of us and conform these expectations to our natural state of life.

For instance, if one person makes a comment about the way we dress for work, we probably won't wear that outfit again. If another makes a comment that we're too shy, we will do whatever we can to prove them wrong. This is where acceptance becomes our greatest obsession, and since we value the opinions of others at times more than our own, we will embrace this expected standard and conform to what is deemed acceptable by others.

Fear of Rejection

When we experience rejection, we can have a difficult time getting back to normal. No one likes being told 'no,' therefore rejection can linger in our minds for as long as humanly possible.

When we don our masks because of this fear, it is a way to protect our heart and spirit from experiencing the same feelings again. When we are rejected, we can feel shame and guilt around it and might even beat ourselves up because of it.

"I should've said it in a different way."

"I shouldn't have given them such a high cost… they probably would've said yes."

"Why did I have to go and open my mouth? Maybe things would've turned out differently."

If we experience rejection on a continual basis—for instance, in our job—we will wear our masks to build resilience and persistence. We will tell ourselves that the next one will be a yes so we can keep going. This fear becomes a motivator to wear our masks as they help us move forward, even though we may feel anxious inside.

We might also use our fear of rejection as a motivator to create a different persona with our masks to ensure we don't get hurt again. We might present ourselves to others with no emotional attachment to the situation and behave in a way that society expects us to. In my experience, this fear is rooted in our need to belong to a particular group of people. We'll don a mask of confidence or of popularity so we can feel valued, appreciated, and seen rather than feel isolated and different from the crowd.

Fear of Vulnerability

When we experience the other fears that are mentioned, the fear of vulnerability comes along for the ride. It can be difficult to express our feelings to others, especially if we fear that we will be judged, criticized or rejected because of them so we tend to keep quiet. As a child, we might've been taught that showing vulnerability is a sign of weakness, therefore we'll put up an emotional wall that is difficult to break down, no matter how hard we hit it. This fear can cause distress in our relationships as well as in the way we communicate. The emotional wall could be the mask we wear as a way to protect ourselves from potential judgment. Being vulnerable and opening ourselves up to others also takes a ton of trust and courage, therefore, when we're not used to being that open or we have difficulty trusting others and letting them in, this fear becomes the motivation we need to remain closed off and don our masks.

When the fear of vulnerability is in its prime, our masks become not only the shield but the full armor that helps us remain in control of our emotions, actions, and behaviors. It is with our masks that we feel comfortable and emotionally stable. They keep us composed and indifferent to any situation that might arise that makes us think otherwise about how we feel.

For instance, when you break up with a partner, it can be mentally and emotionally taxing. However, if you've experienced multiple breakups, it can close you off from having another relationship in order to spare the pain and emotional consequences like the others. If you find yourself getting close to someone again, you'll immediately put on the mask of emotional protection, so you don't allow yourself to be vulnerable again. Embracing this fear, though, and using it as a motivator, does have its consequences. It can stop you from receiving worthwhile relationships, and it can keep people at a distance—it's as if you have a ten-foot pole between your heart and the person you want to get close to. It is important to remember that although it can take time for you to break your emotional wall down and learn to trust again, the relationships you experience because of it can be extraordinary.

Societal Expectations and Mask Adoption

Since we were kids, we've followed societal expectations as much as we can. We've adhered to social pressures as teens, followed cultural norms and expectations of our own heritage, and did what we could to fit in and be liked and accepted. If someone told us that we looked great in blue, subconsciously, we would try and wear blue every single day. If someone at school bullied us and said they didn't like the lunch we brought, we would ask our parents to make us a different lunch or ask for money to buy it. Most often, these societal norms and expectations control the decisions that we make and form the identity that shapes our entire being.

So, what are these expectations, and how do they pertain to the masks we hold? They include the following:

Conforming to Cultural Expectations

As we briefly spoke about in Chapter 1, cultural expectations pertain to the specific actions we take, our behavior, the way we look, and what we choose to believe. When our culture is strong in our roots, we will do whatever we can to adhere to what is required of us, so we don't get shunned or suffer from potential judgment or innate criticism from our friends and family.

For example, there are certain cultures that are required to conform to conservatism, and if anyone in their community oversteps, they could face potential consequences and disapproval. In some cultures, for instance, it is customary to cover your entire face except for your eyes as a sign of respect. In other cultures, your behavior must remain conservative, calm, and collected, and if you step out of this expectation, you're disrespecting your cultural rules. If you are part of a high society community, you are expected to behave in a certain way and are not permitted to step out of your boundaries; this can include the friends you hang out with, the clothes you wear and how you present yourself to others. Because of your culture, you might wear a mask around your family to remain conservative, however, when you're around others, you feel free to take it off and be your authentic self.

Feeling Socially Accepted

For many, many years, the desire to feel socially accepted has been imminent in our everyday lives. We crave external validation, so we try to please people in anything we may do. We desire genuine connection that allows us to be ourselves, and we want to feel like we belong in any circle we are a part of.

Social acceptance is a huge reason why we hold the masks we do. We want to feel more likable and attract others into our circle, so we'll wear our masks to conform to the idea that people might have about us. For instance, if the people we hang around with are more energetic than we are, we will wear a mask of high energy so we can fit in. The mask that we wear is dependent on the ideal version of ourselves that we feel people will accept. This can cause us to hide certain parts of ourselves, especially if these parts are not deemed socially acceptable in our community.

Fulfilling Gender Expectations

These expectations have a lot to do with how you were raised. For example, if your father raised you to become more masculine and dial down your femininity, you will grow up as a person who has difficulty sharing their feelings. You might also grow up feeling uncomfortable with emotionally sensitive people and with those who are more feminine than others. Due to this factor, you will usually adopt a mask that hides your femininity, and you will raise your vibe to be more masculine.

For instance, let's say you have a passion for art, but your father was adamant about you learning about the construction industry so you can eventually become a contractor or laborer. He might even ridicule your gender and say comments such as: "You're a man. Men don't bother with art. They're not that sensitive. It's better if you learn to work with your hands and get dirty." This comment will remain stuck in your mind every time you pick up your drawing pencil. But to conform to your father's expectations of what you *should* be doing, you apply for a construction job and work in the industry, regardless of how much you dislike it. The industry may not be remotely part of who you are, but it is the mask you choose to wear so you can make everyone, including your father, happy. Of course, after a while of "getting your hands dirty," you'll experience an internal conflict because, in the back of your mind, you know that you are not being true to yourself and although you are adhering to the gender expectations, you are miserable, frustrated and annoyed that you have to put on this masked show to please others and be accepted by them.

The thing with conforming to societal expectations is that they challenge you to identify where you are not being your true self and how they are greatly influencing you to continue wearing your masks. I understand the need for social acceptance; however, if you continue to wear your masks, how can you foster an authentic and natural environment that includes genuine connection and togetherness? This is the question we should be asking ourselves the next time we find ourselves trying to conform to specific societal standards.

The Psychological Drivers of a Masked Identity

The thoughts and the beliefs we have in our minds drive the reasons we wear our masks so strongly. These reasons become our motivation to conform to a specific identity that is expected of us or to create a new one altogether in order to feel accepted by society.

As we are aware, our masks act as a canvas for our identity. For instance, if you are female and wear makeup, you use your makeup as a way to adhere to your creative self-expression. You play around with cosmetics and try different looks to see which one suits you best. When you find the one you feel comfortable in, you stick with it for a while and that becomes your signature, the footprint you leave with other's impression of you. Wearing a mask, or many masks at times, is like the footprint we leave in people's minds. If we continue to wear the mask of confidence, that's the impression we leave on others. The psychological drivers of this impression are the ones that make our identity stronger and long-lasting. By motivating ourselves to wear our masks, we can go through a journey of exploration as we learn to express ourselves wholeheartedly. This will help us to navigate uncomfortable situations, understand what we like and don't like about ourselves, and provide a greater perspective of the expectations we set for ourselves to feel accepted.

The Need for Self-Expression

When we wear our masks, it is our way to create a brand for ourselves. It becomes the initial footprint that helps us belong to our desired community. Our masks offer the opportunity to be bold, courageous, and unique.

When we belong to a community, not only do we desire acceptance, but we also desire the ability to seek acceptance in a unique way. Even though we may conform to others' expectations of us, we create the possibility for us to feel accepted in our own skin.

For example, our masks relay certain aspects of our personality to others, even though they may not be the whole truth of who we are. Nonetheless, we use our masks as an opportunity to accept ourselves before anyone accepts us. The masks become the driving force of our own self-perception. If our masks give us the opportunity to promote self-expression, we will wear our masks proudly in front of others and conform to a self-expressed behavior that allows us to shine.

Learning to Adapt

As humans, we are able to adapt to many situations, regardless of our comfort level. In a way, we are a chameleon to the point that we can handle ourselves in any situation, even if it's causing us stress or frustration.

Wearing our masks allows us to adapt and become flexible in situations that require us to conform to certain expectations. For example, if we're usually socially anxious at events, we can use our masks to adapt to the situation by becoming more confident and relaxed. If we have a fear of public speaking, we can generally adapt by wearing a mask of diplomacy and leadership. If you're attending a high-class event, such as a gala or business conference, you can adapt to the dress code and normalize high society behavior, so you don't come off as disrespectful, ignorant, or egocentric.

Adaptation can drive our decision-making as well as our behavior depending on the social situation we're participating in. It may require certain parts of us to be shown more than others—the most important part is to be okay and flexible with what the situation is asking you to do—however, by adapting, you're able to explore different parts of you and turn certain parts of your personality on and off, depending on who you're with, the environment around you, and the expectations you need to conform to.

Empowerment and Self-Control

Understanding this psychological driver has huge benefits for our own motivation. When we wear our masks at a social event, for example, we're able to control our identity, actions, and behaviors. Rather than feel awkwardly shy, we can empower ourselves by creating an identity that is full of confidence, courage, and determination. This identity gives us the strength to move forward and meet people, regardless of how uncomfortable we feel inside.

Our masks give us a sense of control, with the knowledge that we have the power to take them off anytime we wish. We have the power to explore different facets of ourselves and allow those parts of us to shine brightly and hide those other parts of us that are not viable for our own self-expression. We also have the power to break free from societal norms and expectations if we choose to believe they are not bettering our lives, but rather, they are dimming it down.

Past Trauma and Individual Experiences: Shaping Your Masked Identity

When we experience trauma, it can make us think otherwise about who we are and what identity we want to show to the world. It can also give us the desire to hide certain aspects of ourselves, so we don't experience a similar traumatic incident. Of course, that incident can leave a bad taste in our mouth when it comes to showcasing our authentic selves. It also has the power to shape a new identity if we don't enjoy how our other identity represents us.

For example, if we were bullied for several years as a child because of what we look like, we will do what we can, so we no longer experience this type of situation. This includes changing our physical appearance—rather than glasses, we opt for contacts. Instead of short hair, we grow our hair long. We might choose to wear pants instead of the shorts we love wearing. Changing our appearance may not feel aligned to our authentic selves, but we allow our experience with bullying to determine how our identity is shaped.

There are a few other ways past traumas and other experiences can help shape our masked identity. They include the following:

Personal Experiences

Within our lifetime, we go through *many* personal experiences. Some are more pleasant than others, and others teach us a lesson or test our resilience. But here's what I realized. When I understood this, it changed the game for me: each and every experience we endure has a profound impact on the way our identity and personality are shaped.

For example, if you have had your heart broken many times over, chances are, these experiences have left you guarded and emotionally unavailable. When someone tries to get close, you fear that they will break your heart like the others, so you put on a mask of emotional unavailability. This mask doesn't allow you to express your emotions or be vulnerable; instead, it helps you put a wall up in front of your emotions so you can remain on high alert and no longer experience a difficult relationship.

In a way, your identity is shaped by the masks you wear, and they become the means for you to protect yourself and shield your emotions from potential harm. With your masks, you no longer need to face the negative impact of your experiences; instead, you welcome the challenge and invite resilience, strength, and courage.

Traumatic Incidents

There is no doubt that traumatic incidents can have a profound impact on the way your identity is shaped moving forward. If the incident is severely traumatic, it will cause you to wear different masks during social interactions. These incidents also have the power to lose your identity and forget about your overall purpose because you are so wrapped up in the feelings they brought forth, as well as trying to overcome them and heal. They can leave many emotional wounds that can sometimes take a very long time to heal, depending on how traumatic the incident was.

For instance, if you were sexually assaulted as a teen, this incident can cause shame, lack of confidence, and guilt. It can cause you to believe that you cannot trust anyone because all they'll do is hurt you. Because of these feelings, your masks will come on when you're in a relationship or when you are experiencing a situation where you need to trust yourself or others. The amount of emotional scars the sexual abuse has created can change your life drastically and can create an identity you never knew you had before. It can also cause you to live in fear believing that if you let your guard down again, it's only a matter of time before you experience a similar incident.

Healing and Personal Growth

One of the great things about wearing our masks is that we can use them until we are fully healed from any traumatic incidents or personal experiences. We are in control of how long it takes for us to heal, and we can use our masks as much as we would like until we experience freedom from the incidents.

Our masks become an incredible journey for self-discovery, allowing us to reflect on how the experiences have shaped our lives and what we can do to make them better. We're able to reflect on whether we are healing successfully or whether our present experiences are triggering us to fall back in the healing process. In a way, wearing our masks is a therapeutic approach that helps us reshape our identity into someone we long to be. Of course, this can take time, dedication, and commitment to self-soothe and harmoniously heal; if we have the drive and the right masks on, we can turn our feelings of disempowerment into those of empowerment and inspiration. We must also learn to acknowledge what has happened to us so we can accept that it is now part of our lifelong story and the masks we hold. Embracing this fact allows us to develop deeper connections with others and showcase our authentic selves in a way that is deemed self-acceptable.

By choosing to dive deeper into our personal experiences and past traumas, we're able to understand the role our masks play in our lives. We can understand why we wear them and how long we've had them on. It also helps us decipher the various chapters of our story that have played a role in shaping our identity and creating the behavior we know and embrace today. You are also aware that your masks have shaped your identity in a way that helps protect you from the struggles and complexities of life. At the moment, you may not fully understand how your traumas and personal experiences have shaped the masks you wear; perhaps you're currently experiencing a specific situation, but let this section be a reminder for you that your experiences are meant to be embraced, honored, and accepted. They have helped you become who you are today. They have helped create the masks you wear so you can experience healing, growth, and freedom in due time; it is up to you to reflect on this part of your journey with patience, commitment, and dedication, so you can, one day, feel comfortable showcasing your authentic self to the world.

Chapter 3

Types of Masks

Revealing the Different Facades People Adopt

Every single day, we come across people who are unique and have different beliefs and personalities. Every one of our friends and family are completely different from each other, and the way we interact with certain people is different from the way we interact with others. It is important for us to realize that everyone, including ourselves, navigates life wearing different masks depending on the situation, and we embrace different identities and characteristics when we present ourselves to the world. The masks we wear serve a few incredible purposes:

- To shield and protect us from potential harm.

- To create a deeper relationship with our authentic selves.

- To shape the way we engage and communicate with others.

- To motivate us to explore different facets of our identity.

- To explore different ways to create long-lasting relationships.

When it comes to the humanistic approach to fostering profound relationships, it is important for us to recognize the different types of masks that people wear so we can understand their motivation in wearing them.

This chapter is considered the most important chapter of the book. It dives deep into 19 different types of masks that we and others hold. We'll be discussing the role that each plays in shaping the way we interact with others as well as the way we view ourselves.

Each mask that we discuss is among the most common; they encompass unique characteristics and behaviors that drive our interactions and motivate us to entertain this newfound identity. As we begin to understand the driving forces behind the masks and why they are worn, we can create a deeper understanding of human behavior and the intricacies of our self-perception and creative self-expression.

Throughout the chapter, we will encounter masks such as the "pleaser," "perfectionist," "protector," and many others. As you go through each of the characteristics these masks represent, you may resonate with them or notice the people around you who are wearing these masks. This chapter is an important one because it will help heighten your self-awareness and allow you to take notice of the mask you are currently wearing and the mask that others are donning. By examining these masks in detail, you can increase your knowledge and wisdom as you dive deep into the insights they offer, and you can start to pinpoint where the challenges are in relying on them to help you move forward in life. You are able to go on an extraordinary journey of self-discovery and reflect on these masks as you cultivate empathy for yourself and others. As you peel back the layers of society's masked identities, you can take the next step toward creating genuine connections with others as well as stepping into your authentic self.

1. The "Pleaser"

Have you ever experienced a situation where you've put others above your own needs? You did all that you could to please others, even if that meant sacrificing your own well-being in the process just so you can feel accepted.

This is the foundation of the "pleaser" mask. It is the mask that helps us prioritize others, no matter how we think or feel. If you have embraced the pleaser mask, you have difficulty saying no to any task because you don't want to offend people or let them down. You have an overwhelming desire to please people so you can feel accepted by them. Of course, this mask has many downfalls that require you to put others' needs before your own. By doing this, you can feel burned out, stressed, and overly frustrated. People can also use this as an opportunity to take advantage of your help, and because you have a dire need to please them, you will say yes because it is in your nature to do so.

I remember being in school and witnessing *many* people donning the "pleaser" mask. These are especially the people who craved popularity. They would say yes to doing other's homework and even cut class so they could fit in and be accepted into the "popular" crowd. They were also scared to voice their own opinions and assert their creative self-expression for fear that they would be kicked out of the popular group, so they would simply stay quiet. As an adult, they would continue to dedicate themselves to please others by attending social gatherings they don't feel aligned with, or they have no interest in attending. They would also say yes to other projects, even if their schedule is already full, so they don't disappoint their clients or coworkers. Regardless of feeling emotionally and physically drained, they would push aside their own mental health and well-being and press forward for the betterment of others.

2. The "Perfectionist"

If you wear this mask, you make it your mission to be perfect in anything you may do. You strive to be flawless in your actions, physical persona, behaviors, thoughts, and feelings. You are scared to be judged, criticized, or ridiculed, so you don't allow yourself to make any room for error or failure.

Donning this type of mask causes several negative consequences and challenges, which include the following:

- You beat yourself up for making mistakes or failing at something.

- Your self-worth and confidence are called into question.

- If you are not recognized for your achievements, you feel they weren't good enough.

- Nothing you do, be or have is ever good enough.

- Your perfectionism can transfer to your children, which puts unnecessary pressure on them to be perfect.

- If your accomplishments are not 100% perfect, they are not enough, and you push yourself to do better, even if it means that you sacrifice your physical health and mental well-being.

- You fear failure every single day, and because of this, it makes you continually doubt yourself and question your self-worth.

- You're obsessed with perfection, therefore, if the people around you are not perfect, you tend to criticize and judge them for their imperfections.

- You get stressed, overwhelmed, and frustrated from being perfect all the time but you don't allow it to stop you from thriving for the best. Less than the best is not an option because you feel like you're settling.

As I think about the perfectionist mask, I think about my childhood days. We may have been raised by parents who want nothing but the best for us, so they put a ton of pressure on our lives to strive for perfection. If we messed up or experienced failure, they would reprimand us. Rather than appreciate our efforts, they would tell us to "do better" and that they were "disappointed in us." Experiencing this amount of pressure as a child can cause us to grow up feeling like nothing we ever do is good enough and it can transfer into our relationships as well. As perfectionists, we have very high standards and expectations in our relationships, and if they don't meet them, we prefer not to move forward because we feel they are not worth our time.

3. The "Comedian"

When you were in school, you must've had a boy in your classes who was known as the "class clown." They would always poke fun at another's expense and make jokes so the class could laugh.

What people didn't know at the time was that they held the "comedian" mask. Many people who hold this mask tend to be insecure of themselves and question their self-worth, therefore, they use laughter as a coping mechanism to help them get through their journey. If people laugh with them, they won't notice the pain the comedian is experiencing; they use the jokes to hide what is really going on inside of them.

One of the great things about wearing this mask is that you enjoy bringing laughter and joy into someone's life, however, at the same time, you also use laughter as a way to distract others from witnessing your vulnerability or the issues you are currently facing.

For example, you may crack jokes all the time as a way to cope with the loneliness you feel. By making others laugh, it helps deviate your thoughts, so you don't think about your sadness, but rather you bring joy to others.

4. The "Intellectual Expert"

This mask is a way to prove yourself to others. It is greatly tied to seeking external validation and immediate gratification. You might do all that you can to increase your knowledge and wisdom on a particular subject so you can receive recognition and attention from others. Although this may sound like a great trait to have—knowledge is power, as some would say—wearing this mask also comes with a few challenges:

- Your current knowledge is never good enough.

- You seek answers to your questions by looking for them outside of yourself rather than trusting your internal guidance to lead you.

- The learning you experience is never enough; you always need to learn something new, especially if you're not happy with your current situation.

- You always believe you're right about everything; you debate anyone's opinions if they differ from yours. You do what you can to prove them wrong and be known as the expert on the topic.

- You allow your ego to get in the way. If you're not careful, the "expert" mask can turn into the "perfectionist" mask.

For example, when you're at work, you may dominate conversations or start debates about a particular subject to enforce your expertise and knowledge. You might also interrupt others as they're speaking because you don't believe they know what they are talking about, and you know better. This attitude can cause you to ruin relationships with others and can keep you on a higher pedestal to the point that you don't believe there is anyone to challenge you.

5. The "Rebel"

If you're the type that likes to get into trouble and go against the grain, chances are you're wearing a "rebel" mask. You dislike following the rules and usually don't abide by societal norms and expectations. You might use the expression "free as a bird" because you pride yourself in making your own decisions, regardless of what others think. You are very independent, and you crave freedom in many areas of your life.

For example, many entrepreneurs are considered rebels. While most people in their community are conforming to the societal rules of graduating from college, finding a great job, having a family, and settling down, entrepreneurs take a different road. They take the road of *rebelship*, if you will. They abide by the own rules and expectations they set upon themselves; they create their own schedule and work for themselves. They create their own income rather than work for someone else and have their income determined for them. They usually make unconventional decisions and stand by their decision, despite what anyone tries to tell them.

Although wearing a "rebel" mask sounds like an authentic move, especially for those who want to create and build their own lifestyle, there are some negative consequences that are attached to it:

- You are not necessarily open to others' opinions.

- You close yourself off to different perspectives.

- You make your own rules, which can sometimes get you into trouble.

- You have a strong-willed and independent personality which can make it difficult for you to foster genuine connections with others.

- No matter what anyone tries to say, they're wrong, and you make your own path anyway.

- You are big into politics and welcome conflict, so you can prove how independent you are.

- You confront difficult situations head-on without thinking about how they can affect others or whether they will produce a negative outcome.

6. The "Caregiver"

You are the most compassionate one among your friends and family. You care a great deal about putting everyone else's needs before your own. You prioritize others, regardless of how it may affect your own mental and physical well-being. Here's the thing though: you enjoy doing it. You love to ensure that everyone else's needs are taken care of before you consider your own needs.

For instance, you or someone in your family wears this mask every single day. In my case, my mother-in-law holds this mask. Although she aspired to expand her teaching degree and begin teaching elementary school kids again, she decided to care for my sister-in-law's children instead. Since my sister-in-law needed help and couldn't find care for her children while she and her husband were at work, my mother-in-law let go of her aspirations and decided to become their full-time caregiver and has been doing it for many years. Prior to that, she put her dreams and aspirations aside and offered to care for our children as well when they were younger. She enjoyed helping out and did all that she could to support us (and my sister in law) in our own endeavors.

While this sounds like a very compassionate personality, the "caregiver" mask also comes with a few negative connotations:

- You have difficulty adhering to your own boundaries as the caregiver. Very similar to the "pleaser" mask, you have difficulty saying no.

- If you don't prioritize your own needs, such as your self-care routine, you can feel easily overwhelmed and frustrated, which can lead to severe burnout.

- You can eventually hold a grudge or resentment against others for holding tightly to the "caregiver" mask to the point that you neglect your own dreams and aspirations.

- This mask gives many people the opportunity to take advantage of your help and support and overstep your boundaries.

- You will feel unfulfilled later down the road, knowing that you haven't accomplished many of your goals, so you might beat yourself up for being so compassionate.

7. The "Adventurer"

If you hold this mask, it is because you crave excitement and unique experiences. You enjoy spontaneity, and the wind is your lifelong compass. If things feel boring in your life, you prefer to switch up your routine for something more exciting. Chances are, you pick up a new hobby, quit your job randomly for one that feels more exciting or participate in activities where you experience an adrenaline rush, such as skydiving or bungee jumping. You may even spend all your money spontaneously because you enjoy the thrill and the risk it brings you.

Those who hold this mask usually have the travel bug. They crave new and exciting experiences that create a new stamp in their passport. They enjoy heading to different destinations where they learn about unique cultures; they don't steer away from trying unique food that they are not used to. Most often, those who wear the "adventurer" mask are often called a wanderlust.

For example, there are many entrepreneurs who call themselves digital nomads. They enjoy the nomadic lifestyle of never staying in one place for more than a few months. They enjoy the lifestyle adventure brings them, and they thrive on the idea of learning new things that help make their life exciting.

With this mask, though, the following issues can present themselves:

- You lack stability and groundedness. You are so used to "flying by the seat of your pants" that you have difficulty sitting still in one place for a while.

- Being an adventurer, although usually exciting and different, can feel like a lonely and exhausting journey, especially if you don't have anyone to experience it with.

- When you're not being adventurous, life can feel boring and mundane.

- Your adventurous spirit can cause people to think of you as unprofessional and a constant procrastinator because you have difficulty staying in one spot. You need to always be on the go.

- You might lack fulfillment in your everyday life if you're not experiencing excitement all the time. This can cause you to let go of long-term relationships and make spontaneous decisions without thinking about the long-term implications.

8. The "Victim"

At least once in our lives, we experience wearing the "victim" mask. We blame others for our mishaps and have difficulty taking responsibility for our own actions. We rarely accept accountability and find it easier to blame others instead. We usually feel powerless and feel like nothing is going right in our lives, no matter how hard we try to make things better. Anytime we're in a conversation with others, we bring the conversation back to ourselves in an attempt to make others feel sorry for us and hold compassion for our situation. When we are having an argument with our partner, rather than hold ourselves accountable for our own wrongdoings, we blame them and resort to making them feel sorry for ourselves. At times, those wearing the "victim" mask are master manipulators; they can manipulate any situation to their advantage, so they are not called on for their mistakes or failures.

For example, those wearing the "victim" mask usually experience a scarcity mindset. The two words in their vocabulary are "Why me?"

"Why did this happen to me?"

"What did I do to deserve disrespect?"

"What's wrong with me?"

"Will I ever be enough?"

"Will people ever love me for me?"

If you experience a scarce mindset, for instance, you always feel like there isn't anything good in your life. You always complain about all the things you do and don't have. You blame others for your lack of success. You constantly compare yourself to others and perhaps blame them for not reaching the next level. You never have enough money and always complain about your financial struggles to anyone within earshot. You might even complain about your external environment and attribute it to the reasons you haven't reached your desired success yet.

Wearing the "victim" mask and embracing this mentality can cause a few different challenges:

- You have difficulty creating long-term relationships because no one wants to hang out with someone who complains all the time.

- You feel stuck, never moving forward because you cannot see the light at the end of the tunnel.

- You don't trust yourself to move forward, nor do you trust the universe's plan for your life.

- Your decisions are inconsistent because you don't feel that anything is working.

- You give up too easily.

- You are constantly sad, frustrated, and upset about life.

- You bring negative energy wherever you go.

- Rather than find ways to move forward successfully and positively, you stay stuck in a victimized bubble, blaming others for the actions you take or don't take.

9. The "Protector"

Wearing this mask allows you to be a bodyguard of sorts. You feel the need to protect your friends and family from potential harm. You will do anything to ensure their safety, even if it means sacrificing your own well-being. You don't think about yourself when protecting those closest to you; their safety always comes first.

For example, if a burglar breaks into your home when you're sleeping, your immediate reaction is to protect your family, no matter the costs. You will even go to great lengths to protect your pets. You don't think about potentially harmful consequences at that moment; the only thing you're thinking about is ensuring that they walk out of the situation safely.

While wearing the "protector" mask can be a good thing, it also has the ability to overstep your boundaries. While keeping your friends and family out of harm's way is a noble thing, it is also important that you think about your own safety in the process. Someone once told me, "If you are always thinking about protecting others, who is going to protect you?" As you embrace this mask, I encourage you to think about how you would answer this question.

10. The "Chameleon"

In essence, this mask is about having the ability to adapt to any given situation that you are presented with. You are very good at blending into different groups and fitting in during social interactions. You can be an introvert and an extrovert at the same time. You can be the "life of the party" and switch to being the homebody anytime the situation calls for it. Wearing this mask allows you to modify your behavior, interests, and beliefs to feel accepted, acknowledged, and seen.

A great example of the "chameleon" mask is an actor or performer. They have the ability to adapt to various roles, even though they are completely different from each other. They're able to act in a movie in one project and a TV show in another and perform in both roles successfully.

As a relatable example, you may have an opportunity to be the keynote speaker at an event that draws a unique crowd, one that you're not used to speaking to. But, by learning to adapt your speech to reflect the audience's interest, you're able to give an impeccable presentation that keeps your audience engaged.

During most situations, being a chameleon is great, however, it can present a big challenge if you do it often. You can have difficulty finding your unique identity. It can feel challenging to express your authentic self and be creative with your self-expression if you're always adapting your behavior to fit others' needs and interests. You must remember that although you hold the "chameleon" mask, it is important to find your own unique way of doing things so you can also allow your authenticity to shine in the process.

11. The "Optimist"

This is a great mask to adopt. When you wear this mask, you always see the light at the end of the tunnel. You see the glass half full as opposed to half empty. You do what you can to obtain a positive disposition wherever you go, and you make it your mission to inspire others to achieve their greatness and reach their ultimate potential. You enjoy maintaining a positive outlook on life, even when you experience challenges or trials that make you think otherwise.

If you're a life coach, you are usually very optimistic. You challenge clients to become the best versions of themselves and you give them hope and encouragement. Even when you're experiencing difficult challenges yourself, you find a way to come out on the other side full of positivity, knowing that you have the power to overcome any obstacles that come your way.

People will look to you for your optimism because you usually have encouraging advice to give them. This can be a good and a bad thing. It's great to have a positive attitude all the time, but when you are having a bad day, it can be hard to speak with someone about it and for them to take you seriously because you are usually very positive. Optimism, at times, can feel like a lonely journey and can feel like you are not allowed to experience any negative emotions; because while you are a positive light for others, other people may not reciprocate, and it can be difficult for you to process your emotions on your own.

12. The "Admirable"

When you wear this mask, you seek constant external validation from others and do what you can to project an image that is worthy of admiration. Most of the time, you believe in your own power and your ability to achieve your ultimate potential, and you do the things you do so you can receive immediate gratification.

When you experience challenges, you give it your best effort so you can be recognized and admired by others. You usually pursue achievements not necessarily because you want to but because you want to prove your worth to others.

For example, let's say you are participating in an obstacle course. The only thing you can think of is the praise you will receive when you win the game. You push yourself, even through the most challenging feats, so all the recognition you can get. If you don't win, you might beat yourself up and believe you didn't try hard enough. In your opinion, if you want to feel truly admired by everyone, you need to be the best at everything you do. Let's not mistake this mask for the mask of perfectionism—they are very different. You achieve your accomplishments as a way to prove your worth to others and their recognition of your efforts can be sole proof that you know what you are doing and are admired for it.

However, as you work to prove your worth, you feel empty. If you're not feeling validated all the time, it can make you question your worth and whether what you're doing is truly worth it. Even if you're working on a passion project, if someone is not appreciating your efforts and validating your greatness, it can make you feel like you want to give up because you are not being supported or admired.

13. The "Nonchalant"

When you wear a "nonchalant" mask, you have a neutral attitude toward any situation. You are usually calm, cool, and collected. You emotionally detach yourself from any situation that requires you to express emotion. While wearing the mask, you don't appear affected by the experience, or you feel indifferent and impartial toward all parties involved. If you're feeling nonchalant toward a situation, it could be because you're not allowing yourself to be vulnerable; perhaps you've been hurt in the past, and you don't want to feel that way again, so you use a nonchalant attitude as a way to protect yourself and defend your vulnerability.

For example, let's say you experienced a partner's infidelity more times than you can count in the past. These experiences can cause you to build an emotional wall in front of your vulnerability, so you don't get hurt again. As this wall is up, you meet someone you truly care about, but because of past incidents, you are emotionally attached to the relationship. When your partner tries to have a vulnerable conversation with you, you ignore it or detach yourself from it and change the subject. These types of conversations might make you feel uncomfortable, so you do what you can to show that you are unaffected by the conversation.

One of the downfalls of wearing this type of mask is that you don't allow yourself to create deeper relationships for fear that you will get hurt again. When it does come time to share your emotions with others, it can feel difficult to fully express yourself in fear that you may be judged or criticized. Because of this, you keep your feelings to yourself and take them as a grain of salt and brush them away as if they don't matter.

14. The "Competitor"

Throughout your life, there are individuals who tend to be overly competitive. They have to win at everything, and if they don't, they beat themselves up because of it, and then they go after the win again and again until they beat everybody. They constantly compare themselves to others to see who has the best—the most expensive car, a big house, better kids, a hotter partner, more money, a better career, fitter body, better leadership skills, and more knowledge—everything feels like a competition.

When I think of the "competitor" mask, I can think of one character from a popular 90s TV show to help explain the power of this mask: Monica from Friends. Throughout each episode, she is extremely competitive and wears the competitive mask proudly. It is within her humanistic nature to be the best at everything she does. For instance, there is a specific episode where she is planning a huge Thanksgiving dinner for her friends. In this episode, she makes it a game to compete with herself to see who made the better Thanksgiving dinner: the version of herself last year or who she is today.

However, apart from a few downfalls of wearing this mask, there is one that stands out: those who usually wear this mask constantly fear failure. They continually compare themselves to others, including their friends and family, and if they fail at something, they immediately question their worth or whether they were good enough to complete the task. This can cause your relationships to suffer as your super competitive streak can make you neglect everything else in your life but winning.

15. The "Martyr"

As a martyr, you sacrifice yourself for others and stand by your beliefs. Very similar to the "protector" mask, selflessness is your strong suit. If you have strong beliefs, you will stand by them, no matter what—even if it means you're supporting them alone. This is the same for your sacrifice for others. You will do anything for those you care about. If they're in trouble, you prefer to sacrifice yourself to defend them. It gives you joy and purpose to be able to do this for them and to remain steadfast in what you believe.

For example, let's say you have very strong religious beliefs. You will do whatever you can to stand by these beliefs, even if it means your life may be in question. You advocate and stay strong if you're feeling threatened and victimized. Your beliefs (and the people you care about) are important to you, no matter what the costs.

Wearing the "martyr" mask can cause you to overstep your own boundaries and neglect your physical, mental, and emotional well-being for the betterment of others. It can also cause you to feel alone in this journey, especially if no one agrees with your beliefs. Being selfless is appreciative, but you might struggle with establishing your ground rules and knowing when it's enough.

16. The "Free Spirit"

You embrace individuality, creative self-expression, and freedom and don't follow societal norms and expectations. You always refer to yourself as someone who is "free as a bird." You love the idea of spontaneity and following your own path. You excel at self-leadership and decide for yourself rather than have others decide for you.

One of the greatest qualities you possess when wearing the "free spirit" mask is that you tend to be very calm, cool, and collected. You take everything with a grain of salt and make decisions from a calm and neutral point of view. If people tell you one thing, but it doesn't feel aligned, you will create your own path and decide to do something different. If everyone else around you is conforming to societal expectations, you'll reject them and do the opposite.

I have many friends who wear the "free spirit" mask all the time. Everyone tells them to get a job for more financial stability, but they always choose to work for themselves. As free spirited individuals, they love the freedom of being able to wake up anytime they want and go on vacation without having to request time off from their boss.

Wearing the free spirited mask has many advantages, but there are also a few disadvantages. They include the following:

- Lack of stability. As a free spirited entrepreneur, you don't have stable clients or income. This can cause your business to go downhill if you're not committed to taking action every day.

- Difficulty forming long-lasting relationships. If you are always traveling, for example, there isn't much time to meet and get to know people.

- It can appear irresponsible. Spontaneity and going with the flow can make people believe you don't know what you want and that you don't care about anything or anyone.

- You might notice you're also wearing the "rebel" mask, which can cause you to follow trouble because you believe in the sense of freedom so much.

17. The "Influencer"

Do you create an impact in people's lives? Do you inspire and influence them to become better versions of themselves and to follow their dreams? Chances are, you're wearing the "influencer" mask. This is usually worn by people who have a mass following and influence people wherever they go.

For example, many politicians are considered influencers in their industry. There are also world-renowned makeup artists who have made a name for themselves on social media as an influencer. They have hundreds of thousands, sometimes *millions* of people, following them and what they represent. Many celebrities are also known as influencers, as people are inspired by the impact they're creating on the big screen. There could also be local influencers as well who create a substantial impact in your community. Perhaps they're news announcers or a media team—they keep you up to date with their creative ideas and newsworthy stories, and their journalistic approach keeps you interested and creates a significant impact in your life.

While being an influencer sounds great, it also comes with a few downfalls:

- You might have difficulty maintaining your authenticity. People love influencers because they are authentic and promote creative self-expression. As you generate a bigger following, you might start to lose your authenticity and create a new identity profile without meaning to. Being an influencer can get to your head sometimes, and you might lose sight of why you're an influencer in the first place.

- You wrestle with maintaining your privacy. As an influencer, people want to know more about you and get to know the real you, so your privacy is no longer secure.

- You need to be careful that you don't experience public scrutiny. As an influencer, everyone is watching every move you make. As you become more popular, you might have media personalities following you, even if you go to the grocery store. You must be careful about what you say and what you do, as it might be taken out of context.

- Seeking external validation is high on your radar. As an influencer, you become more popular, and your following grows anytime someone talks about you with others. This can cause you to produce content where you seek validation from your audience. If they don't respond or they don't like it, it can make you lose your sense of self-worth and confidence.

- You struggle with meeting everyone's expectations. Your audience can sometimes expect a lot from you, and if you don't meet their expectations, they can stop following you at a moment's notice. This can put a lot of pressure on your mental health and on the actions that you take.

18. The "Seductress"

A seductress, although mainly used to describe flirtatious women, attracts many people with their charm. They have a charismatic personality that can make them an influencer for potentially the wrong reasons. At times, they use their looks to get what they want, and they are known to manipulate others with their sexy demeanor. Sometimes, women don't even know they're wearing the "seductress" mask—this part of their personality comes out naturally.

For example, think about when you were in school. There was always someone who was considered the most popular girl in school. She had a huge following, mostly boys, and was usually liked by many kids in your grade. She was also considered very pretty and wore designer clothes, and came from a wealthy family. She knew how to manipulate people, especially the boys, to get what she wanted, whether it was money, food, or other items.

But with this type of personality and mask-wearing capabilities comes a few negative qualities:

- The struggle to form genuine and authentic relationships. As a seductress, you don't know if your relationships are real or if they're spending time with you because of what you look like or what you have.

- Many people with the "seductress" mask usually lack self-confidence and have low self-esteem. You might use your looks and materialistic items to make up for what you don't have and how you're feeling internally.

- Your attitude can sometimes draw the wrong crowd to you. You might want to form genuine relationships, but certain people can be spending time with you for their own personal gain.

- People can have high expectations of you. As a seductress, you can be considered perfect sometimes, which can cause you to be afraid of showing your imperfections. You might feel judged or criticized for showing anything but perfection.

- You might have difficulty creating an authentic profile. Since people have certain standards about who you are, it can feel difficult to understand what's truly authentic about you. You might struggle with your own unique identity and self-expression.

19. The "Loner"

Wearing the "loner" mask classifies you as the lone wolf. You prefer to be by yourself most of the time. Rather than go out and meet new people or attend social gatherings, you prefer to stay at home in peace and quiet. You are very independent and will go on vacation or to the movie theater on your own.

To some degree, many introverts consider themselves loners. They are homebodies who find solace remaining in their own company rather than in the company of people they just met. Chances are, you know a few introverts (perhaps even yourself) who exhibit these traits.

A few other traits that come with naturally being a loner include the following:

- Despite the name, it can be a very lonely journey. In the beginning, wearing the loner mask can exhibit many positive traits, but after a while, solitude can also feel a bit boring and sad.

- Shyness can also come with being a loner. You might have severe social anxiety that makes it difficult for you to meet new people; because of this, you adopt the "loner" mask as a way to avoid feeling shy, nervous, and uncomfortable.

- You lack the ability to form deep connections with others. Because you are so independent and prefer to work alone, this can make it difficult to create genuine relationships as well as expand the connection on a deeper level.

- You don't believe in "following the leader." This belief and your independent nature, can cause you to take a path alone most of the time.

I hope these masks have given you an idea of the different facades used by yourself and others. Depending on the circumstance and for their own personal gain, people use their masks as coping mechanisms in order to overcome an uncomfortable situation. I encourage you to keep these masks in mind so you can become aware of the ones that you hold and the ones that others adopt when they interact with you. Gaining a better understanding and becoming aware will help you create and foster deeper relationships with others.

Chapter 4

Seeing Beyond the Masks

Techniques for Uncovering Authenticity

In Chapter 3, we elaborated on several masks that people can wear on a daily basis. By now, you understand how prevalent it is for people to carry their masks anywhere they go, and at a moment's notice, they can put it on immediately to overcome an uncomfortable situation.

As you've gone through that chapter, and any others before it, perhaps you had questions arise in your mind:

- If I wear this many masks, how do I know when to take them off?

- How long have I had them on?

- How will I know when my masks are off, and I am free to show my most authentic self to the world?

This last question, in particular, is what this chapter is about. This chapter is about uncovering and shedding light on your authenticity. It's about determining when it is the right time to take off your masks and be exactly who you are in all your authentic glory. We all want to connect with others and build relationships with them based on trust, togetherness, and deep inspiration and impact, but most often, our masks don't allow us to do that. How can our masks show us in our most authentic light? The possibility doesn't make a whole lot of sense. And although the masks we wear have significantly impacted our lives in many ways, it is time to uncover the tools and strategies required to lift the veil and uncover our deepest selves to the world.

I don't know about you, but I would rather share the full authentic scope of who I am from the beginning rather than create a perfectly curated version of ourselves in order to make a great impression and then have to answer questions later about why we've changed.

There are a few key points that we'll be discussing in this chapter:

- How to shift your perspective and implement effective tools and strategies that help you reconnect to your most authentic self.

- How to create the internal willingness to see beyond the masks people wear and express an interest in exactly who they are without immediately raising judgment.

- Why specific tools such as active listening, empathy, and non-judgment are important in order to foster and nurture meaningful relationships.

- How to enhance and strengthen your emotional intelligence so you learn to create a balance between your internal thoughts and your emotions—they're meant to work together.

- Why self-awareness is an integral part of mask-wearing and how you can use it to break free from the many masks you hold once and for all.

By the end of the chapter, you will feel empowered knowing that you are equipped with the tools and strategies you need to grab hold of your authenticity so you can create genuine connections and dive deeper into understanding others on a level beyond their masks.

The Art of Discernment: Recognizing Authenticity

In my opinion, it takes a keen eye to recognize when people are being genuine or promoting false claims. At times, most people are very good at faking authenticity; false personification comes naturally to them.

This section is about learning how to recognize when people are being authentic. Although it can prove to be a difficult task, with self-awareness, the willingness to dive deeper into the connection, and your ability to be open to different perspectives, you can begin to discover when people are being raw and authentic. At the same time, you can decipher when people are falsely misrepresenting themselves and perhaps even call them out to promote the importance of authenticity.

This is an important section because it will allow you to create a deeper understanding of the people around you. By diving deeper and choosing to see beyond what the mask represents, you can form genuine connections and foster profound relationships based on authentic connections.

It's not every day that we get the opportunity to see beyond the mask; most people leave it on and entertain their facade for many, many years. It is when they get home they feel free to truly be themselves. By then, they are alone with no one to judge, criticize or ridicule them. They can be as free and as bold as they want. But my question to you is this: How can you form genuine, authentic connections with others if you are too afraid to let go of your masks? If you are too afraid to let people into your authentic world?

According to Merriam-Webster, authenticity is "the truth of one's own personality, spirit, or character". It tends to be quite a complex concept. To truly value your own authenticity, you need to reason with yourself and be okay with showcasing your full expression to others. You must be okay with expressing yourself in a way that is unique to you rather than being a carbon copy of other's actions, words, and behaviors. Authenticity is also meant for you to push beyond what is expected of you in society and to let go of pleasing people or asking for approval and validation.

I understand that it may be difficult to recognize who is being authentic and showing their true selves to you, but this section will help you alleviate the stress of trying to recognize authenticity.

The following are effective strategies that you can implement so you can start decoding people's authenticity:

Understand Nonverbal Communication

Nonverbal communication consists of a few cues that are not overly visible to the naked eye. It takes a keen eye and intentional self-awareness to be able to pay attention to these cues and decipher whether a person is being authentic.

Nonverbal gestures consist of the following actions:

- crossed arms
- whether they are making eye contact

- how they cross their legs
- facial expressions
- tone of voice
- gestures
- posture
- appearance

For example, you may notice that the person you're speaking with is not making eye contact with you; that is a sign that they could be nervous or hiding something. If their arms are crossed or have slouched posture, they could be feeling uncomfortable or bored in the situation. However, if they are smiling or they are sitting in the receiving position (palms facing up with their legs uncrossed), they could be feeling at ease and comfortable with who they are. By learning to observe how they nonverbally communicate, you can increase your awareness and understanding of whether they are being real or not.

Practice Active Listening

We'll speak more about this in the next section; however, active listening plays an important role when trying to recognize a person's true self.

Active listening is a skill that everyone should master. It's about fully engaging with the person you're speaking with; not just listening to what they're saying but paying full attention to their tone of voice and the words they use. The authenticity cues tend to be quite subtle during a conversation, so by being intentional with the engagement, you can pick up on whether they are being real or if they're using a mask to speak. You can also make it a point to repeat back what they're saying so it shows that they are being seen and heard, which can also allow their authenticity to shine.

Trust Your Internal Guidance

To recognize authenticity, we must learn to trust our intuition. Our intuition is a powerful tool that can decipher right from wrong. When we're speaking with others, our intuition can tell us whether they are being authentic or if they are wearing a mask.

When we are wrapped up in conversation, it can be difficult to listen to our intuition, but it is crucial to remain intentional so we can sense others' genuineness. This guidance can make us aware of whether the stories they tell us about themselves are fact or fiction; it can also tell us whether they are hiding something or telling us the full truth. Although our intuition can provide us with valuable insights into a person's deeper self, I encourage you to combine this trust with another effective tool or strategy. If we're not used to listening to our intuition, we might get the facts wrong and create unnecessary conflict unintentionally. As you practice being more intentional with listening to your intuitive guidance, you are able to practice sound judgment and receive clarity.

Look For Inconsistency or Loopholes

When someone is not being authentic, you can usually tell because their stories don't match their actions, behaviors, words or values. Instead, they are telling you what you want to hear in order to potentially avoid conflict or risk you finding out their inner truth or intentions.

For example, they might share things with you that sound empowering and inspiring, however, behind closed doors and with others, they are completely different people. They may tell you that their main values are trust and kindness, however, you might notice their actions that tell you otherwise or are inconsistent with what they are telling you. It is important to recognize when this happens, so you can decide what to do moving forward. Perhaps you choose to call them out on their inauthenticity because they may not even recognize it within themselves. Trusting your intuition is an effective strategy to pair with this as well as active listening.

Remember to Be Patient and Open

To recognize authenticity, the first step is to remember that patience and openness are key. So is dedication and commitment to be receptive. If you experience snap judgment based on an initial statement or reaction, it could be detrimental to your relationships.

For example, even though first impressions are important, you might encounter someone who is nervous or uncomfortable with meeting others or engaging in conversation. This initial behavior doesn't mean they are being inauthentic or hiding something; in retrospect, these attributes could be purely authentic and the truth of who they are. During the initial impression, they could also come off as ignorant, prideful or cold. They might very well be wearing a mask in order to protect themselves from potential judgment or hurt.

Rather than rush to determine authenticity, take your time and be patient during interactions. Recognizing others' truth can take several conversations that require you to practice active listening and learning more about them, their beliefs, and values. Instead of rushing the process, give them the space to share and be themselves. Create a supportive environment that demonstrates that they can be comfortable showing up authentically and in the full truth of who they are.

Empathy and Active Listening: Connecting on a Deeper Level

There is power in showing empathy and being intentional with how you listen to others during conversations. Empathy and active listening are two traits that should be acknowledged and embraced when trying to recognize authenticity. When you have these down to a science, so to speak, you're able to practice non-judgment when first interacting with others or when you're engaging in an ongoing conversation. They're especially important when you want to create a deeper relationship with others and connect on a more profound level.

So, what is empathy? Empathy is "the action of understanding, being aware of, being sensitive to, and vicariously experiencing the feelings, thoughts, and experience of another". In other words, it is when you are able to experience the feelings of another as they are experiencing them in real time. It takes an acquired skill to master empathy. There are many people in this world who are excellent at demonstrating empathy for others. They have an extraordinary sense of judgment and can sense when someone is sad, frustrated, or excited, even from a stranger.

As we practice empathy with others, we give them the opportunity to release their masks and step into their authentic selves. We give them the space to express their creative self-expression and naturally be who they are meant to be. Rather than judge them, we support them and give them time and space to remove their masks when they feel the time is right. By doing this, we also show them compassion and help empower them rather than disempower and criticize them for being themselves.

Active listening is also an acquired skill. Most people will speak and engage in conversation without fully hearing what the recipient is saying. At times, they speak without thinking. According to Verywell Mind, active listening is about "going beyond the actual words being spoken, but instead, trying to understand the meaning behind them".

When you combine both empathy and active listening, you're able to connect with others on a deeper and more profound level.

Practicing Empathy

There are a few ways you can start practicing empathy during your next conversation. They include the following strategies:

- See things from the other person's perspective. Step outside yourself for a moment and put yourself in their shoes. How do you think they are currently feeling about the situation?

- Create a non-judgmental atmosphere. Set up a

space for others to safely express themselves without holding bias toward them. Give them the opportunity to be fully heard, acknowledged, and seen.

- Acknowledge how they're feeling. As they speak their truth, validate their emotions, and hold their feelings in high regard. Telling them you understand how they're feeling can greatly help, and they'll feel appreciative and understood. They will continue to feel safe in expressing the authentic truth of how they're feeling.

- Look for commonalities in your stories. As they share, search your own story and experiences for highlights that can resonate with them and demonstrate that you understand how they're feeling. This can help you create trust with the other person to the point that they will continue to share authentically without holding anything back or wearing their masks. It can also help deepen the conversation so you can foster and nurture the connection.

Practicing Active Listening

As you master the art of active listening, you can implement the following tools and strategies to help increase trust and authentic connection:

- Be present and mindful during the conversation. In other words, don't be on your phone or distract yourself with something else. Be present and intentionally engage.

- Maintain eye contact with the person you're speaking with.

- Recognize their nonverbal communication to become aware if what they're saying is true. You can usually tell if they're being truthful by understanding how they're communicating with their body and tone of voice.

- Fully engage with them. Ask them questions that don't only require a "yes" or "no." It shows you're fully listening, and you're interested in getting to know them on a deeper level.

- Repeat back what the person is saying. By doing this, you are showing them that what they say matters and that you value their opinion. It also shows them that they are being seen and heard.

- Refrain from judgment. Instead of criticizing them, practice non-judgment. Be slow to judge and quick to listen. Give them the opportunity and space to share their truth.

- Refrain from giving them advice immediately. Sometimes, all they require is someone to listen to them.

Practice Non-Judgment

To truly implement the art of empathy and active listening, it is imperative you practice non-judgment. As humans, we are very quick to judge others, even before we get to know them. Because of this, the people we are immediately judging are very quick to put on the many layers their masks represent as a way to protect themselves from further criticism.

To help create a safe and trusting environment where others can shed their masks and connect to their authenticity, the following strategies are a few practices that you can implement:

- While engaging with the person, **keep an open mind** as you practice active listening.

- **Use nonverbal communication.** By agreeing with them and showing them that you understand where they're coming from by using your body language, you can cultivate empathy and mindfulness. For instance, you can express interest by maintaining eye contact and leaning in toward them. To show that you understand, you can nod your head or cock your head to the side in acknowledgment.

- **Demonstrate that they can trust you** by keeping what they tell you to yourself. Confidentiality cultivates trust, empathy, and understanding from both parties. It also gives them the reassurance that you won't share their vulnerabilities with others unless they give you permission to do so. If they know that they can trust you, they will continue to be open and authentic with you.

- **Encourage authentic self-expression** without judging them. If they're wearing a mask, they are usually trying to protect their inner truth from potential criticism or ridicule. Give them the space to be themselves and to express themselves naturally so they can feel comfortable taking off their masks.

Developing Intuitive Insights and Cultivating Emotional Intelligence

Emotional intelligence, as described by Verywell Mind, is "the ability to perceive, interpret, demonstrate, control, evaluate, and use emotions to communicate with and relate to others effectively and constructively".

In other words, practicing emotional intelligence is not only about understanding others' emotions; it's also about the ability to balance, control, and express your own emotions at the same time. It's as if you're killing two birds with one stone.

Many of us have the ability to do one or the other, so it takes a certain level of mastery to combine both emotional capabilities. It's not impossible; it simply takes effort, practice, and commitment to defy the odds and master emotional intelligence.

So how can you practice emotional intelligence, so you become better at it? It takes a few key concepts that include the following:

Become Self-Aware

Self-awareness is the bread and butter of emotional intelligence. When you understand what triggers you, the emotions you're currently feeling, and what motivates these emotions, you'll have a greater understanding of others.

There are a few tools that you can implement immediately to begin cultivating self-awareness:

- **Self-reflection.** When you're experiencing a series of emotions, take some time to self-reflect. Understand why you're feeling that way and what is triggering you to stay in this energy. It can help if you close your eyes and focus on your present moment awareness. This allows you to look deep within yourself and reflect on your present circumstance.

- **Journal.** In my own experience, journaling is an extraordinary tool to help practice self-awareness. Some people have multiple journals that are set aside for specific experiences. For example, a gratitude journal can help remind you of all the things that you currently have in your life that you should be grateful for. A self-love journal can help you understand how to create a deeper connection with yourself. Journaling is a tool used to create moments for self-reflection and to help you gain insight and clarity.

- **Be open to constructive criticism and feedback.** You may not be self-aware of your patterns or limiting beliefs, but by being open to feedback, others can help you become aware of the areas you need to work on in order to achieve personal growth.

- **Be mindful.** Engaging in mindfulness practices, such as silent or guided meditations, can help you cultivate extraordinary self-awareness. These practices allow you to observe your thoughts and emotions from an outside perspective rather than come from a place of judgment. If you're also feeling overwhelmed and overthinking about everything, mindfulness practices can help clear your mind and allow you to focus on the things that need your attention.

Recognize Others' Emotional Signals

The ability to recognize others' emotional signals is a big part of cultivating strong emotional intelligence. At the beginning of the chapter, we discussed the importance of nonverbal communication and signals; understanding others' emotions are part of their nonverbal cues.

The following includes a few techniques that you can pay attention to when learning to recognize how others are feeling:

- **Observe their body language.** Notice their facial expressions, how they are standing or sitting, whether they're making eye contact or looking away, and their tone of voice. Do they keep looking away when speaking with you? It could be because they are nervous about something. Is their tone of voice high-pitched or low? They could be excited, or they could be shy and anxious. Are they slouching? They could be bored or uninterested in what you're saying.

- **Understand their mini expressions.** For example, they might have a hint of annoyance in their eyes, but it disappears quickly as a way to hide how they're truly feeling. They might feel sad or angry, so you notice their brow furrowing or wrinkles on their forehead. These expressions are very subtle and, without warning, can disappear without a trace. By catching on to these expressions, you can have an idea of how they're currently feeling.

- **Notice their energy.** You can usually tell how a person is feeling by paying attention to their energy. If they're upset, frustrated or sad, they carry themselves slowly and have a neutral or stagnant expression on their face. If they're excited or happy, their energy is usually vibrant, colorful and infectious. When you're having a conversation, you must pay attention to others' energy. Depending on how the conversation is going, their energy has the potential to shift drastically. By paying attention to these cues, you can get an idea of how they're feeling at the moment.

Unmasking Yourself: The Journey of Self-Awareness

Understanding our own authentic mark in the world takes a certain amount of practice to master. We must be attuned to our own emotions, experiences, self-expression, and the like. As discussed in the previous section, self-awareness is key to unmasking ourselves and understanding our own authentic identity.

In my own experience, cultivating self-awareness is a journey. It takes time, patience, practice, and dedication. We must commit to learning more about ourselves and creating a deep relationship with ourselves full of compassion, empathy, and clarity. Mastering self-awareness is not an overnight process; in hindsight, it can take several months or years to develop this skill. It's like peeling an onion. You must pay attention to the little details that represent the full scope of the onion. There are many layers you need to get through in order to reach the core. Self-awareness is a very similar journey. It's a journey of self-discovery and understanding oneself so we can gain clarity and insight about who we are behind the masks we hold.

There are a few key components we must consider when practicing self-awareness. They include the following:

Reflect on All That You Are

Your life's journey up until this point has many interconnected pieces. They include extraordinary moments of pleasure and fulfillment, relationship faux pas, challenges that you've overcome, successes, failures, life lessons, a-ha moments, breakthroughs, and traumatic experiences.

Whether we like it or not, all of these experiences tie in together and create the person we are today. They are the moments that made us realize how important our values, beliefs, and boundaries are; they are also the moments where we were able to discover a purpose and a passion for something. These experiences helped shape our beliefs and helped us understand what masks we hold and how valuable we are in the world. We must reflect on every single one of these experiences to help us fully comprehend the person we are today and the person we are meant to become.

Use Your Challenges to Identify Your Passion and Purpose

When we are in the process of discovering our purpose and what we're passionate about, we will go through many challenges and obstacles that help tie it all together. In the heat of the moment, we may not realize that it interconnects, but once we overcome our challenges, we begin to reflect on why we experienced them in the first place. These moments help us become self-aware of the way we react to certain scenarios—for instance; perhaps we're excited when we share our life experiences on social media. Perhaps we experience a traumatic incident, and the moment we overcome it, we understand why it happened.

All of these experiences help us gain insight into what brings us passion and purpose. They help us become aware of what we're great at and where extraordinary self-leadership lies. By receiving clarity through the challenges you experience, you will understand what truly matters to you so you can move forward feeling aligned, intentional, and purposeful.

Recognize Your Strengths and Weaknesses

Give yourself a moment to reflect on what you're great at and the areas you need to work on. We must recognize these areas, so we know where to focus our energy as opposed to focusing on an area that we dislike or are not strong at.

It is also important to remember that you don't have to be great at everything. For instance, your partner may be excellent at math, but it just isn't your strong suit—that's okay. The sooner you recognize your weaknesses and become aware of them, the better off you'll be in the long run.

On the other hand, when it comes to your strengths, you can embrace them and leverage your energy, so you become better at it. You might enjoy writing, and you know you're talented at it, so you can leverage it and make your gift stronger by embracing it in various ways. By becoming aware of these attributes, you can start to live authentically and use your strengths to move forward while accepting and acknowledging the areas that require growth and improvement.

Embrace Self-Acceptance

One of the key things about self-awareness is the ability to love and accept yourself for all that you are. You may be overly sensitive or get excited about the littlest things—that's okay. Embrace these attributes for all they're worth.

We all have many imperfections that contribute to our uniqueness. Of course, some of these imperfections, if not all of them, tend to be the culprit of having a love-hate relationship with ourselves. Rather than embrace our flaws, we prefer to put on a mask so we can hide them and never bring them to light. But here's the thing. By hiding them, you do the complete opposite of what this chapter is about: embracing and acknowledging your authenticity.

Unmasking yourself takes three crucial steps:

- acknowledgement
- acceptance
- self-love

Each of these steps ties in together and makes up exactly who we are. By acknowledging our flaws and imperfections, we learn to accept them and fully embrace them. When we do all this, we create a more profound relationship with ourselves based on self-love, self-trust, and self-compassion. We remind ourselves that it's okay that we make mistakes, experience failure, or have weaknesses; as long as we learn to embrace what makes us unique, we can live a beautiful and fulfilling life without our masks.

Challenge Your Limiting Beliefs

When we start to adopt our masks, it is usually because we adopt limiting beliefs first. These beliefs shape our identity, and we grow up, and they become the narrative that we live our life on. They also influence the masks we wear, and they are a clear-cut sign of how we view ourselves.

For example, we might have been bullied for many years during childhood. Although traumatic, this experience has helped shape our identity in the following ways:

- Decreased our self-love and confidence.
- Questioned our worthiness.
- Created beliefs based on others' perception of us.
- Lost our trust and faith in others.
- Created emotional blocks.
- Increased the need to seek external validation.
- Made us socially awkward and anxious.
- Increased other people's immediate judgment about who we are.

All of these points have created limiting beliefs in our mind that reflect in any decision that we may make.

They've shaped the way we think about ourselves and the way we view the world. To further deepen our self-awareness, we must challenge these beliefs so we can let go of the narrators and reframe our thoughts and overall identity.

Promote Authenticity in Your Relationships

I've always believed that in order to maintain authenticity in your relationships, it is important to embrace your own self-leadership first. When we want to strengthen our relationships, the best thing we can do is to become a role model so our partner naturally takes notice.

For instance, as we learn to embrace our own authenticity and lead in that manner, we can be sure that our partner will follow suit. To help with this, we must implement the following tools and strategies:

- **Have open and honest communication.** You mustn't hold anything back. Practice communicating and active listening at the same time. Learn to express your thoughts, values, opinions, and feelings in a way that is authentic, real, and honest.

- **Surround yourself with a circle of trust and influence.** When cultivating authenticity in your relationships, you must surround yourself with people who are willing to do the same.

Surround yourself with people who inspire you, lift you up, and encourage you. Find connections and create an authentic relationship with them where being seen, heard, valued, and appreciated are at the forefront of their priorities.

- **Create boundaries and stick to them.** To foster healthy and authentic relationships, setting boundaries is important for our overall well-being. Set clear expectations from the beginning about how you want your relationship to flourish. For example, set boundaries in the way you effectively communicate with each other, what happens when you experience conflict, when your trust threshold is reached—what happens next? Once these boundaries are set, you must honor and respect them while at the same time having mutual respect for each other's boundaries.

By understanding how to unmask your own authenticity as well as recognize that of others, you can create more profound relationships based on intimacy, deep connection, and unbreakable trust. You can create a bond that is unlike any other and continue to nurture the relationship, so it continues to flourish.

It can take some time to unmask your own authenticity so you can begin to tap into your own potential. As this chapter discussed, it is important you continue practicing self-reflection, compassion, and self-awareness so you can dive deeper into understanding yourself on an authentic level. You can challenge your beliefs, embrace your authentic identity and recognize the opportunities that allow you to remove your masks and let them go for good.

Chapter 5

Building Genuine Connections

Nurturing Meaningful Relationships in a Masked World

Building genuine connections takes a certain level of skill and can be quite challenging, especially if the people you meet wear their masks all the time. In a masked community, it can be difficult to foster authentic connections, let alone nurture them.

As described throughout this book, most people are wearing their masks as a means of comfort, protection, and safety. Some of us don't even realize we are wearing them; we've worn them for so long that it has become part of our lifelong journey of survival. Although wearing our masks can be a good thing in the beginning, it can also hinder the notion of creating genuine relationships with others as well as create barriers when we want to break our walls down.

However, if we learn to be honest, exhibit trust, and are open about our authenticity, just as we discussed in the previous chapter, we have the opportunity to see beyond the masks and build relationships that are intentional, genuine, and meaningful. At the same time, if you exhibit creative self-expression with others and are comfortable with taking your masks off, others can get to know the real you, and you can practice self-acceptance.

As this is the last chapter, we'll be addressing the challenges and opportunities we experience every day in order to build and foster connections. These challenges are ones that we have the power to overcome as long as we are committed and dedicated to prevailing.

In this chapter, we'll also be discussing the importance of vulnerability, trust, and open communication within our relationships. Without these three components, it can be difficult to nurture relationships. They are the puzzle pieces that help create genuine connections and allow you to foster and nurture them with creativity, care, compassion, and unconditional love.

Fostering and nurturing connections without our masks can take some time. We must work on embracing our authenticity every day so we can cultivate self-acceptance and trust as we take the next steps toward removing our masks for good. Of course, there will be many times when you'll want to put them back on as you meet people—remind yourself that it is okay to do so. As you continue to create a connection with others, you will feel comfortable removing your masks inch by inch until it is fully removed.

Although this world is full of masked identities, you have the power to build genuine connections and nurture meaningful relationships as much as you would like. It takes a few steps in the right direction to experience change and transformation in yourself and others. In short, it is a journey. And this journey will help give you insight into a world of empowerment where extraordinary relationships can be created beyond the masks.

Embracing Authenticity: The Foundation of Genuine Connections

We live in a world where our masked identities dominate our authenticity. With our masks, interactions feel a bit made up and superficial; we never really know if someone is being truthful or if they are hiding parts of themselves out of fear. In any case, however, we are making it our mission to seek out genuine connections and create powerful relationships based on trust, openness, empathy, and honesty more than ever before.

Perhaps it's because we now feel lonely, having to put up this masked charade that we spent many years of our lives creating, but now we want something better for our lives. We want fulfillment and meaning in our relationships. But, in order to achieve this, we must engage in our own self-leadership and start peeling back the layers so our authentic selves can shine. When we do this, we become a role model for others to also do the same; this is when genuine connections can start forming.

To embrace our authenticity, we must have the courage to show up for ourselves. We must learn to accept every part of ourselves, including our flaws and imperfections. We must be honest about who we are and where we came from. Embracing and accepting our authentic selves is about expressing full honesty about how we're feeling with others without holding anything back. At times, we might make others uncomfortable when we are open and vulnerable, but that could be because they are also learning to remove their masks so they can live in authentic freedom.

One of the great things about embracing authenticity is that you have the opportunity to be real with others wherever you go. You could be expressing yourself on social media and sharing about self-love and acceptance while acknowledging your flaws—that is a bold move that constitutes tremendous personal growth. It might not feel easy to allow others to see us in our most vulnerable state, but I can tell you that it is a *very* liberating experience. Demonstrating your authenticity in this way offers you the opportunity to create meaningful relationships. They are able to witness your vulnerability while, at the same time, feeling inspired to share their own. Immediately, a seed has been planted that helps you connect with others on a deeper level.

Honor Your True Self

There are many different facets that your authentic self represents. You have weaknesses, strengths, flaws, imperfections, and a unique personality. When you wear your masks, perhaps you show your strengths, but you keep your weaknesses hidden. Perhaps you embrace one of your flaws but dislike the others.

Regardless of your current circumstance and how you're feeling at the moment, you must learn how to honor your true self. This honor comes from a few instances:

- Forgetting about potentially feeling judged.
- Letting go of external validation.
- Forgetting about societal expectations and paving your own lane.
- Understanding that you cannot please everybody, no matter how hard you try.
- Making up your own rules at times, even if it means going against the grain of everybody else, as long as you follow your own path.
- Embracing everything that makes up who you

are.

Honoring your true self can take some time, practice, and patience. If you've worn your masks for a very long time, it's not that easy to let them go. It's a matter of fully accepting yourself for who you were and embracing the person you are now.

To create authentic connections with others, it is important you embrace a journey of self-discovery. Take the time to get to know yourself on a deeper level. Be kind to yourself and understand what your values, passion, and purpose are. It is obvious that you are a work in progress, and every day, you are learning and growing, but it doesn't take much to honor yourself and celebrate how far you've come.

Remove the Masks

When we wear our masks, we demonstrate a part of us that we want the world to see and essentially let go of the rest. When we're by ourselves, however, these parts are prevalent, and we are free to be exactly who we are; there is no one around to judge us.

By removing our masks, we become courageous in our endeavor to seek out genuine connections, even if that means letting people into the shadows of our flaws and imperfections.

When we remove our masks, a few things can happen:

- We create the opportunity to build authentic relationships.

- We become completely transparent about our stories, intentions, and how we're feeling.

- Our connections feel more genuine and truthful.

- We practice honesty with ourselves and others.

- We remain truthful and listen to our intuition if something doesn't feel right.

- We learn to trust others enough that we allow them to see our imperfections wholeheartedly.

- We promote self-love and acceptance and create a deeper relationship with ourselves.

- We create boundaries and hold ourselves accountable to remain steadfast.

I encourage you to challenge yourself to have the courage to remove your masks. Practice mindfulness during conversations and remember to be present and engaged. If you notice that you're putting your mask back on, practice self-reflection and understand the triggers that caused you to take a step back and reevaluate whether removing your masks was a good thing.

Live In Alignment With Your Authentic Self

Living in alignment is a phrase that is unheard of by many people. When I think of this statement, I think of the following:

- balance
- peace
- serenity
- extraordinary experiences
- harmony
- authenticity
- self-expression
- unique identity

Now, when it comes to your authentic self, living in alignment is about creating a harmonious balance between your values, beliefs, and actions. It is also about creating a balance with your energy and ensuring it matches up with your values and your actions.

Alignment is about creating choices in your life based on the decisions you have made and remaining steadfast in these decisions because, internally, they feel like they are the next move. It involves making choices that are aligned with your authenticity and identity, regardless of societal norms and expectations. These choices are the ones that matter to you and no one else.

Alignment can be powerful because it helps you tap into your inner power and reflect upon that of your most authentic self. When you start aligning your choices and the decisions that you make with your authenticity, you attract relationships of a similar nature. For instance, if it feels aligned to move to a tropical destination, and you act on that alignment, you'll meet people who desire to make a similar decision that you can wholeheartedly connect with.

When you wear your masks, however, it can be difficult to understand what feels aligned for you. You may think that a certain situation or experience feels right, but perhaps it feels right because of the mask you're wearing, not because it is part of your true self. Mastering self-awareness can help with understanding what feels aligned to you and your authenticity and what is in alignment with the masks you wear.

To start living in alignment with your most authentic self, I encourage you to create the space you need to help you identify your values and beliefs. What do you value most in your relationships with others and with yourself? Is it trust? Commitment? Faith? Whatever your values are when it comes to connecting with others, focus on the actions you take that align with your values. For example, if you value trust, ensure that you are also making decisions and taking action in a way that demonstrates that you can be trusted.

Embrace Your Vulnerability

When we are tapping into our authenticity and removing our masks, embracing our vulnerability is key. We may have grown up where acting vulnerable is unheard of; perhaps we were raised by parents who were afraid to show up for themselves and publicly express their emotions. They may have been told somewhere along the way that expressing how they're feeling is never a good thing, so they were taught to keep it in a tight little container in their mind.

However, learning to let go of this belief and allowing your vulnerability to shine through in your interactions is the first step to showing up for your true self. It is about showing up and demonstrating that you are human and that you also have fears, insecurities, and dreams. By learning to express your vulnerability without fearing judgment, you allow yourself to be heard and fully seen, which in turn, helps you create and foster genuine connections. It reminds you that although there are challenges, you have the power to overcome them with grace, resilience, and determination, as well as with the support of others.

It may not be easy to be vulnerable, especially if you are used to emotionally shutting down when you experience situations that feel uncomfortable—it can lead to potential rejection, failure, or judgment—however, there is such courage in coming out of your shell in this way.

To put this into practice, the best thing you can do for your own personal growth is to find opportunities where you can be vulnerable, even if the steps are small. For example, if you're having a bad day, feel comfortable sharing your thoughts and feelings with your partner or a trusted friend. If you are excited about something, share it with those closest to you. By taking a leadership role when it comes to your vulnerabilities, you open the floor to others to do the same, and it can create a harmonious ripple effect of deep bond and connection.

The Power of Effective Communication: Fostering Trust and Openness

Effective communication has never been more apparent than it is today. In order to foster deep connections with others, we must learn to communicate effectively. I've always believed that it's better to listen before you react; this is where the power of active listening becomes crucial during interactions.

If you immediately react without fully comprehending what the other person is saying, it can lead to unnecessary conflict and can go deeper into the conversation than originally intended. Both parties can walk away in a frenzy, believing that neither has been seen, heard or valued for what they were trying to say. To avoid these situations, effectively communicating your message is crucial for both parties involved.

To communicate effectively, it requires three key components:

- openness
- trust
- understanding

When these factors are taken into consideration during conversations, you will walk away from the interaction with a positive outcome and mutual agreement. It is through mastering these skills that you can experience a sense of belonging, unconditional love and support, and a deep connection with others. It is also through these skills that you can help others remove their own masks and build on their authentic foundation. You create a safe space for all parties to share how they're authentically feeling, what they're thinking about, and what's potentially triggering them. It allows you to engage in true understanding and empathy rather than try and create an authentic relationship with someone who refuses to remove their masks.

The following techniques are ways that can help you master effective communication while fostering trust and openness at the same time:

Be Fully Present

As you are aware by now, active listening is a fundamental component to learning how to communicate effectively. Active listening is about releasing all distractions and being fully present in the conversation.

I understand that we can get easily distracted during a conversation, especially if our phone is within earshot or a notification pops up. Maybe our children need our assistance, or there's a knock on the door. However, when you're having a conversation with someone, you must find ways to be fully present and engaging. Rather than check your phone the moment a notification pops up, place it face down and give your undivided attention to the speaker. This demonstrates respect and interest in what the speaker is saying. It also ensures that their opinion is validated, appreciated, and understood.

Being fully present during interactions is also not only about active listening. It also includes the way you use your nonverbal language to communicate so the speaker is aware you're acknowledging them. You must also refrain from offering judgmental comments that you feel would help the situation, but in essence, it will only make it worse. Rather than have preconceived notions about what they're saying, keep an open mind as you engage with them. Think before you speak. Ask yourself: Is what I'm saying helpful or kind? Does it inspire them? Is it truthful, or am I creating unnecessary assumptions?

Demonstrate Your Understanding and Empathy

It can be difficult for many of us to remove our masks and express our vulnerability. It can make us feel uncomfortable and perhaps think twice about keeping them on. To promote effective communication in your conversations, you must demonstrate empathy. As empathy can take some time to fully master, it is also a skill that can come out naturally during conversations.

For example, when I'm having a conversation with someone, I take the time to get to know them. I try to put myself in their shoes so I can understand how they're feeling, and then I drive the conversations from there. When people are expressing their vulnerabilities to you, take a moment to understand where they are coming from. This can help build trust and allow them to fully express themselves to you with openness, honesty, and authenticity.

I also encourage you to release your perspective of the situation. By immediately sharing your perspective, it can come off as judgmental and condescending. Instead, take a moment to reflect on their own understanding of it. How are they feeling? Why are they feeling triggered? How can you support them and validate their emotions while being empathetic to their situation?

When people feel vulnerable during conversations, it is usually because they want to get something off their chest. To create a deep connection with them where they feel they can trust you and come out of their shell, it is important you step into the conversation offering immediate understanding and empathy. By doing this, they will feel more comfortable being themselves every time they speak with you, which can lead to a unique bond between both parties.

Cultivate Trust and Openness

In any relationship, trust is the foundation to make it work effectively. If people don't feel comfortable removing their masks and expressing their authentic selves to others, it is usually because they have difficulty trusting others to be themselves. Perhaps they experienced multiple situations in the past that lost their trust in humanity. These experiences closed themselves off and created a barrier between their authentic self and their masked persona. Because of this, they keep their guard up, so they protect themselves from potential hurt, shame, or judgment.

So, to cultivate trust in your relationships, you mustn't force it and allow the trust to come naturally. By remaining consistent when communicating and by always being honest, you open up the space for others to trust you with their own vulnerabilities. You open up the space to engage in insightful conversations that rely on effective communication as well as being true to ourselves.

Being reliable is also the main key to having a trusting relationship. When you lack integrity, people lose their trust in you, and it becomes the evidence they need to continue wearing their masks. However, if you are open and act in complete honesty, they will begin to trust you and share their authentic selves over time. It is important to remember that building trust is not an overnight success. Depending on the situation, it can take weeks, months, or sometimes even years to fully gain someone's trust. This is why it is vitally important to always act with integrity with what you're saying and the actions you choose to take.

The Role of Vulnerability and Emotional Intimacy

When wanting to deeply connect with others, we must first understand what this entails, as it can mean several things. First, it's a matter of building a foundation based on vulnerability and intimate connection. Second, you must learn to release the fear of judgment and allow yourself to emotionally connect with yourself and others. This helps you balance your emotional intelligence, so it deeply aligns with your actions, behaviors, and thoughts. Third, it is apparent that you need to let go of any fears and insecurities you may have as you build that connection. Perhaps you experience the following thoughts:

What if they don't like me?

How can I prove myself to them?

What do I need to do to be part of their circle and feel a sense of belonging?

What if what I have or who I am is not enough?

What if they judge me before they get to know me?

What if they reject me?

There are many "what if" questions such as these that can determine our fate when it comes to solidifying and nurturing relationships. These insecurities can make us feel like we cannot trust anyone with our authenticity. They can make us feel like we're better off being alone without having sound relationships. So, although there are challenges to being vulnerable and emotionally intimate with others, you must remind yourself that you have the power to overcome these challenges and come out on the other side having relationships that are fulfilling and meaningful.

With that being said, there are a few things you can do to help foster the connection and create a space where vulnerability and emotional intimacy are encouraged:

Create a Non-Judgmental Space

When people don't feel like they can trust others to be themselves, it is likely they feel immediately judged before they even have a chance to prove themselves. It is important to create a non-judgmental space where they can feel safe and nurtured. This space can give them the comfort they need to speak the truth and be themselves. It allows them to feel a sense of acceptance and belonging where their opinion is respected and highly validated. They don't need to think about whether they are being judged or criticized; in retrospect, they can feel the opposite—seen, heard, and unconditionally supported.

Let Go of Perfectionism

When we feel the need to be perfect in everything we do, it can take us further away from our authenticity and unique self-expression. Perfection can make us feel like we're not permitted to be vulnerable in fear of what others may think.

We must remember that we are only human. Sure, we might make mistakes and experience failure—that's okay. We might have many flaws and imperfections that makeup who we are, but it is important we remind ourselves that they come with our unique, authentic package. By accepting and embracing these flaws and learning to let go of perfectionism, we can find a way to forget about our insecurities and simply be who we are. This allows others to do the same, which creates a safe space for genuine and real connection. Letting go of perfectionism creates a unique bond that no longer involves wearing a mask, but instead, we are allowing our authentic self to shine in our interactions.

Cultivate Emotional Intimacy

What is emotional intimacy? According to a specific article on ChoosingTherapy.com, emotional intimacy refers to "the closeness and connection between two people who feel safe and secure with one another".

In other words, it involves sharing your vulnerabilities, deep thoughts, and desires in order to emotionally connect with others. Being emotionally intimate creates a sense of trust and safety in another's presence.

For example, in order to have a loving and trusting relationship, being emotionally involved with your partner is key to making it work. I'm sure there are times when you have emotionally intimate conversations with your partner about life, career, or your long-term visions and aspirations. At the same time, they share their own with you, and you create a trust factor where each of you feel emotionally comfortable sharing the deepest desires of your heart. It is an opportunity to express your deepest vulnerabilities with the knowledge that you are in a safe and trusting space to be yourself. You know you are being seen and understood by your partner, which makes you feel safe and held. This helps you create a space where you can feel supported, accepted, and deeply connected to each other.

The Challenges of Vulnerability and Emotional Intimacy

Now that we've discussed how vulnerability and emotional intimacy can play a role in our lives, we must be aware of the challenges these factors can also present. They include the following:

- We can experience fear, rejection, and judgment. These insecurities can be hard to let go of and can be detrimental when wanting to be vulnerable.

- It requires us to step outside our comfort zone and into the unknown, which can also present a fear that can stop us from deeply connecting with others. By stepping outside our comfort zone and into our inner truth, we open the doors to potential judgment and criticism. This can be an overwhelming fear, especially if we're not used to being vulnerable. If this fear is strong, it can be very challenging to open ourselves up to others.

- We might regret it, especially if our vulnerability is not reciprocated.

- It can take some time for us to feel comfortable expressing ourselves authentically. We mustn't rush the process; instead, take small steps and put it into practice. Eventually, it will feel easier to be ourselves to the point that our masks are no longer needed.

The Rewards of Vulnerability and Emotional Intimacy

Where there are challenges, there are also huge rewards. Here are a few of them:

- You have the opportunity to create a deeper bond and connection with others.

- You can create a sense of belonging and acceptance.

- You can promote empathy and understanding, which allows you to strengthen the connection and help people feel seen and validated.

- Conversations are more effective and can relate well to the journey. By being vulnerable and authentically expressing your emotions, you can relate to others, which helps them open up more to you.

- It helps create a deep level of trust, integrity, and faith in each other.

- It creates a supportive space where emotional intimacy and self-expression are encouraged.

- By being vulnerable and sharing your heart, you can foster personal growth and become a better version of yourself, which helps you release your insecurities and, in turn, embraces your imperfections.

- You promote extraordinary self-awareness by recognizing and accepting the moments where you are vulnerable.

Cultivating Empathy, Compassion, and Respect

Society as we know it today is full of masked identities. It can be difficult to form genuine connections with others that are not only surface-level connections. We have become incredibly wrapped up in how people see us on social media, at work, and in other instances that we feel the need to entertain this masked persona everywhere we go. How can we cultivate empathy and compassion for others when we don't know if they are being genuine or putting up a face in order to please us? There is no doubt that our masks have created a barrier in our lives that defers us from fostering authentic connections. Instead, we live our days only creating surface-level bonds that get us in the direction we need to go, but in the end, we feel lonely and have difficulty trusting anybody or being vulnerable.

However, by learning how to cultivate empathy and offer compassion for others, we are able to garner respect and exhibit it at the same time.

The following are various ways that you can embark on an empathetic and compassionate journey with others:

- **Perform random acts of kindness.** By showing your support for others' projects and endeavors, you can start creating empathy toward their needs. In the previous sections, we spoke about empathy in combination with understanding; however, I'd like to shed a bit more light on what it means to be empathetic. While putting yourself in other's shoes so you can understand where they're coming from is important, it is also crucial that you show your support in other areas. Show your support in ways that encompass empathy by offering your ear when they need advice or by offering encouraging and uplifting words that empower them.

- **Show that you care about others.** By showing compassion toward others' needs, you acknowledge that what they're going through is validated, and they have your unconditional support. Your partner or another family member might come to you for support and advice; rather than express judgment, give them the opportunity to freely express how they're feeling. Once they're finished, you can respond with love, warmth, and kindness. You can offer them empowering advice where it's needed, but the most important thing is to show that you care about what they're going through.

- **Compassion through self-leadership.** When you want to demonstrate compassion for others, you must become a role model that they can relate to. This allows them to trust you to understand what they're going through. Offer yourself compassion when it's required, as it will help you balance and regulate your emotions.

- **Validate and honor different perspectives.** You must remember that not everyone's perspective will be the same as yours. Ensure that you honor different points of view, as this can help you with your own personal growth. You can learn from others while at the same time validating their opinion.

By now, you know how to create and foster genuine connections that can last a lifetime. Although it does take time, patience, dedication, and commitment, it is encouraging to know that these relationships can be worthwhile. Together, you can build a foundation based on authenticity, unique self-expression, and commitment to supporting each other, with or without your masks.

Conclusion

Today, I remove the mask that hides me from who I am. I find my voice, sending a clear message to the universe about what's important to me. In return, I experience more good in my life. –Rev. Jane Beach

As you gather from this book, creating genuine connection takes three things to put into action:

- courage
- intentional effort
- being open to new possibilities

Every day, we have the opportunity to become better at who we are. We have the opportunity to create extraordinary decisions that stand the test of time and that allow us to embrace our authentic selves and showcase them to the world.

As I've mentioned throughout this book, it may not feel easy to remove our masks and keep them off for good. There will be many times when we'll put them on again—more than likely when we're meeting new people. We must understand that although we choose to wear our masks for a time, we have the power to remove them anytime we wish.

These chapters are meant to constitute growth and personal evolvement. Although we live in a world where masked identities are predominant, we have the insatiable opportunity to look beyond the masks and create a deeper connection with others that is bound to last a lifetime.

Some of the highlights from this book include, but are not limited to:

- The importance of being present and mindful. To create connections where empathy is imminent, active listening must be part of your daily interactions. Release distractions and be present in the moment.

- By cultivating self-awareness, you begin to understand the areas that require effort and focus. You are able to reflect on triggering moments as well as create a balance with your emotional intelligence.

- We can only go so far with creating superficial surface-level connections. Eventually, it will feel lonely, and we'll crave deep connection and bonding with others. Rather than continue to use our masks to create these connections, how about we find a way to remove them and share our authenticity instead so we can start forming meaningful and fulfilling relationships that make a difference.

- We must recognize when our connections don't feel aligned with our own behaviors, values, and beliefs. By becoming aware of this, we can take the steps required to step into alignment and plant seeds with the right people.

- Although there are many challenges to being vulnerable, there are also many rewards that you can celebrate. They include achieving personal growth, creating a deeper bond with others, living in alignment with your authenticity, promoting unique self-expression, and creating a deeper relationship with your self-love and acceptance.

- In order to build a sustainable relationship that you can foster and nurture, you must hold space for non-judgment. This allows others the opportunity to open up to you and allow their authenticity to shine.

- Self-leadership is a key component to creating and fostering powerful relationships. Cultivate your own personal growth and learn the lessons you need to so you can teach others how to do the same by the actions you take.

- You must honor your own authenticity and offer it the respect it deserves. When you fully love, accept and embrace yourself, regardless of your imperfections, others will reciprocate, and give you the same attention.

- There are so many masks that we described in Chapter 3. Which ones do you resonate with the most? Is it the "victim" mask? The "seductress?" The "perfectionist?" Perhaps all of them? Take some time to reflect on which masks you hold, become self-aware, and find ways to remove them one by one.

- There is no such thing as perfectionism. We may have been brought up to believe that it exists, but we must release the need to be perfect and focus on embracing and accepting our imperfections.

- There will always be societal norms and expectations we are required to conform to. It is up to us if we choose to be a follower by wearing our masks or decide to pave our own unique path by removing them and expressing our own identity. This decision will determine how we live our life moving forward.

There are so many other highlights I can mention, but this gives you an idea of why it's important to remove your masks and be yourself. Allow this book to be the guidance you need so you can take the next step toward embracing your unique identity. If you take anything away from this book, I encourage you to take this quote by Oscar Wilde: "Be yourself. Everyone else is taken."

I appreciate your time, effort, and dedication toward releasing your masks and embracing your authenticity. Use the tools and the strategies I shared in this book to help you release your own masks. Every time you put them on again, refer to this book and read parts of it again. Allow it to serve as a reminder for you that just as you were able to remove them the first time, you can do it again and again, as many times as needed.

I also encourage you to share this book with the people in your life who are strongly holding onto their own masks due to fear and other insecurities. This is the book that can help coach them through their own struggles while learning to embrace their imperfections at the same time. You no longer need to wear your masks; have the courage to take them off so you can create the connections you've been longing for.

Thank you for joining me on this journey.

BRIAN BASTERFIELD

If you enjoyed the book, I would be incredibly thankful if you could take just 60 seconds to write a brief review on Amazon, even if it's just a few sentences.
Your communication helps me create even better content for you.

A Free Gift to The Readers

Thank you for choosing to read this book. I hope you find it insightful and practical.

To enhance your experience and provide additional value, I've included the following material at no extra cost to you:

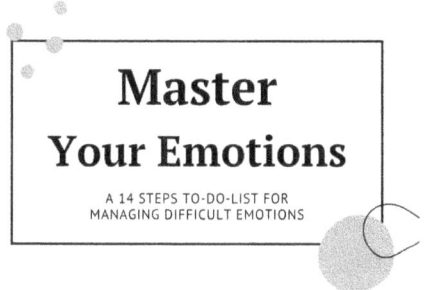

This supplementary content offers valuable insights related to managing your emotions.

To access your bonus material, please scan the QR code below:

Thank you for your support, and enjoy your reading!

References

Ackerman, C. (2018, August 6). What is self-expression? Positive Psychology.

https://positivepsychology.com/self-expression

Ackerman, C. (2020, April 1). What is self-awareness? (+5 ways to be more self-aware). Positive Psychology.

https://positivepsychology.com/self-awareness-matters-how-you-can-be-more-self-aware

A Conscious Rethink. (2022, October 20). What is self-reflection and why is it so important? A Conscious Rethink.

https://www.aconsciousrethink.com/10258/self-reflection

A Conscious Rethink Team. (2023, June 14). 15 truths to help you overcome your fear of being judged. A Conscious Rethink.

https://www.aconsciousrethink.com/12596/fear-of-being-judged

Adler, L. (2021, June 6). 10 deceptive masks narcissists wear. Toxic Ties.

https://toxicties.com/masks-narcissists-wear

Admin. (2020, May 21). The masks we wear. Mind and Body Works.

https://mindandbodyworks.com/the-masks-we-wear

Agathangelou, F. (2015, May 19). How to overcome your fear of rejection to improve self-esteem. HealthyPlace.

https://www.healthyplace.com/blogs/buildingselfesteem/2015/05/how-to-overcome-your-fear-of-rejection

Akre, K. (2023, June 20). Nonverbal communication. Encyclopedia Britannica.

https://www.britannica.com/topic/nonverbal-communication

Aletheia. (2022, September 29). Do you suffer from the fear of rejection? (Read these 9 inspiring tips). Lonerwolf.

https://lonerwolf.com/fear-of-rejection

Bailey, J. & Rehman, S. (2022, March 4). Don't underestimate the power of self-reflection. Harvard Business Review.

https://hbr.org/2022/03/dont-underestimate-the-power-of-self-reflection

Bansal, S. (2023, June 14). 12 powerful networking tips for introverts at virtual and IRL events. Braindate.

https://www.braindate.com/networking-tips-for-introverts

Barreto, M. (2021, January 5). How does fear affect our social lives? Psychology Today.

https://www.psychologytoday.com/ca/blog/identity-and-community/202101/how-does-fear-affect-our-social-lives

Baumeister, R. F., & Leary, M. R. (1995). The need to belong: Desire for interpersonal attachments as a fundamental human motivation.

Psychological Bulletin, 117(3), 497-529

Beer, J. (2020, March 5). The inconvenient truth about your "authentic" self. Scientific American.

https://blogs.scientificamerican.com/observations/the-inconvenient-truth-about-your-authentic-self

Bcrnc, E. (2011). Games People Play: The Basic Handbook of Transactional Analysis. Tantor.

Berne, E. (2022). Transactional Analysis in Psychotherapy: A Systematic Individual and Social Psychiatry. Licensing Management, Inc.

Bickford JM, Coveney J, Baker J & Hersh D. (2018, July 12). Self-expression and identity after total laryngectomy: Implications for support.

Psycho Oncology, 27 (11), 2638-2644

Boogaard, K. (2023, May 10). Hear us out! Active listening is worth the effort. Atlassian.

https://www.atlassian.com/blog/communication/active-listening

Bowden, M. (2023, February 26). Overcome your fear of being judged. Mark Bowden Hypnotherapy.

https://www.markbowden.com/overcome-your-fear-of-being-judged

Braidwood, D. (2019, November 11). The masks we wear: Authenticity in the workplace. LinkedIn.

https://www.linkedin.com/pulse/masks-we-wear-authenticity-workplace-david-braidwood-mba

Brodsky, A. (2022, January 20). Communicating authentically in a virtual world. Harvard Business Review.

https://hbr.org/2022/01/communicating-authentically-in-a-virtual-world

Brooks, A. (2021, October 28). The disguises we wear every day. The Atlantic.

https://www.theatlantic.com/family/archive/2021/10/emotional-mask-hide-feelings/620506

Brown, B. (2010). Gifts of imperfection: Let go of who you think you're supposed to be and embrace who you are. Hazelden Publishing.

Buggy, P. (2017, August 11). Non-judgment: What is it? And why does it matter? Mindful Ambition.

https://mindfulambition.net/non-judgment

Burrowes, N. (2014, April 11). Think authenticity is about being honest and open? Think again. The Guardian.

https://www.theguardian.com/women-in-leadership/2014/apr/11/real-meaning-authenticity-leadership

Celestine, N. (2021, November 13). How to begin your self-discovery journey: 16 best questions. Positive Psychology.

https://positivepsychology.com/self-discovery

Chernev, A., Hamilton, R. & Gal, D. (2011). Competing for Consumer Identity: Limits to Self-Expression and the Perils of Lifestyle Branding. Journal of Marketing American Marketing Association, 75 (3), 66-82. 10.2307/41228597.

https://www.researchgate.net/publication/228960160_Competing_for_Consumer_Identity_Limits_to_Se lf-Expression_and_the_Perils_of_Lifestyle_Branding

Cherry, K. (2022, January 26). 5 key emotional intelligence skills. Verywell Mind.

https://www.verywellmind.com/components-of-emotional-intelligence-2795438

Cherry, K. (2023a, February 22). Types of nonverbal communication. Verywell Mind.

https://www.verywellmind.com/types-of-nonverbal-communication-2795397

Cherry, K. (2023b, February 22). What is empathy? Verywell Mind.

https://www.verywellmind.com/what-is-empathy-2795562

Cherry, K. (2023c, March 10). What is self-awareness? Verywell Mind.

https://www.verywellmind.com/what-is-self-awareness-2795023

Cherry, K. (2023d, March 11). What are the Jungian archetypes? Verywell Mind.

https://www.verywellmind.com/what-are-jungs-4-major-archetypes-2795439

Cherry, K. (2023e, May 2). Emotional intelligence: How we perceive, evaluate, express, and control emotions. Verywell Mind.

https://www.verywellmind.com/what-is-emotional-intelligence-2795423

Christian, L. (2021, March 22). How to be your authentic self: 7 powerful strategies to be true. SoulSalt.

https://soulsalt.com/how-to-be-your-authentic-self

Clark, D. (2014, August 15). Networking for introverts. Harvard Business Review.

https://hbr.org/2014/08/networking-for-introverts

Coursera. (2023, June 15). What is active listening and how can you improve this key skill? Coursera.

https://www.coursera.org/articles/active-listening

Cuncic, A. (2019, July 19). 5 tips to manage the fear of being judged. About Social Anxiety.

https://www.aboutsocialanxiety.com/fear-of-being-judged

Cuncic, A. (2022, November 9). What Is Active Listening? Verywell Mind.

https://www.verywellmind.com/what-is-active-listening-3024343

Daniere, E. (2019, September 2). Communicating emotions. Psychology Today.

https://www.psychologytoday.com/us/blog/talking-emotion/201909/communicating-emotions

Davenport, B. (2022, September 14). What is a free spirit personality? 27 of the top traits. Live Bold & Bloom.

https://liveboldandbloom.com/09/personality-types/free-spirit-personality

DeCesare, H. (2020, August 14). 5 steps to challenge limiting beliefs that hold you back. Your Tango.

https://www.yourtango.com/experts/hilary-decesare/steps-challenging-limiting-beliefs-that-hold-you-back

Definition of authentic. (2023, June 27). Merriam-Webster.

https://www.merriam-webster.com/dictionary/authentic

Demartini, J. (2020, November 24). Expressing your authentic self. LinkedIn.

https://www.linkedin.com/pulse/expressing-your-authentic-self-dr-john-demartini

DeWall, C. N., Baumeister, R. F., & Vohs, K. D. (2008). Satiated with belongingness? Effects of acceptance, rejection, and task framing on self-regulatory performance.

Journal of Personality and Social Psychology, 95(6), 1367-1382

Dundon, E. (2018, May 17). To live with meaning, shed your masks. Psychology Today.

https://www.psychologytoday.com/us/blog/the-search-meaning-after-age-50/201805/live-meaning-shed-your-masks

Edelstein, B. (2018, June 2). Authenticity and intimacy. Psychology Today.

https://www.psychologytoday.com/us/blog/authentic-engagement/201806/authenticity-and-intimacy

Ellevate. (2019, October 7). How I learned to love networking as an introvert. Forbes.

https://www.forbes.com/sites/ellevate/2019/10/07/how-i-learned-to-love-networking-as-an-introvert/?sh=578762a52bcb

Ellis, T. (2021, February 18). Overcoming fear of rejection: The complete guide. Apotheosis LLC.

https://dontpanicdothis.com/fear-of-rejection

Emotional intimacy: What it is and how to build more of it. (2023, February 6). Choosing Therapy.

https://www.choosingtherapy.com/emotional-intimacy

Empathy. (2023, June 27). Merriam-Webster.

https://www.merriam-webster.com/dictionary/empathy

Empathy exercises: How to be empathetic in an increasingly online world. RingCentral Blog.

https://www.ringcentral.com/us/en/blog/empathy-exercises

Eurich, T. (2018, January 4). What self-awareness really is (and how to cultivate it). Harvard Business Review.

https://hbr.org/2018/01/what-self-awareness-really-is-and-how-to-cultivate-it

Fancied Facts. (2019, February 20). How does fear affect society? Medium.

https://fanciedfacts.medium.com/how-does-fear-affect-society-cc3cd156ad54

Fletcher, J. (2022, October 28). 11 personality masks we wear. Psych Central.

https://psychcentral.com/health/the-masks-we-wear

Fritscher, L. (2023a, March 10). How to overcome a fear of rejection. Verywell Mind.

https://www.verywellmind.com/what-is-the-fear-of-rejection-2671841

Fritscher, L. (2023b, April 11). The psychology of fear. Verywell Mind.

https://www.verywellmind.com/the-psychology-of-fear-2671696

Gardner, W. L., Gabriel, S., & Lee, A. Y. (1999). "I" value freedom, but "we" value relationships: Self-construal priming mirrors cultural differences in judgment.

Psychological Science, 10(4), 321-326

Goffman, E. (1959). The presentation of self in everyday life. Anchor.

Grubbs, L. & Geller, G. (2021, March 8). Masks in Medicine: Metaphors and Morality. Journal of Medical Humanities, 42, 103–107.

https://doi.org/10.1007/s10912-020-09676-w

Gupta, K. (2019, December 27). Embrace the practice of self-acceptance to embrace yourself the way you are. Youth Incorporated.

https://youthincmag.com/embrace-the-practice-of-self-acceptance-to-embrace-yourself

Gupta, S. (2022, September 14). How to embrace self-acceptance. Verywell Mind.

https://www.verywellmind.com/self-acceptance-characteristics-importance-and-tips-for-improvement-6544468

Heatherton, T. F., & Polivy, J. (1991). Development and validation of a scale for measuring state self-esteem.

Journal of Personality and Social Psychology, 60(6), 895-910

Heine, A. (2023, May 18). 100 reflection questions for personal and career growth. Indeed.

https://www.indeed.com/career-advice/career-development/reflection-questions

Herrity, J. (2022, September 30). What is self-awareness? (And how to increase yours). Indeed.

https://www.indeed.com/career-advice/career-development/what-is-self-awareness

Hilton, E. (2020, July 8). 3 steps to challenge your self-limiting beliefs. Welldoing.org.

https://welldoing.org/article/3-steps-challenge-your-self-limiting-beliefs

Hodge, J. (2022, June 24). What is self-expression and why is it so important? Counselling Directory.

https://www.counselling-directory.org.uk/memberarticles/what-is-self-expression-and-why-is-it-so-important

How do you balance authenticity and professionalism in your stage presence? (n.d). LinkedIn.

https://www.linkedin.com/advice/1/how-do-you-balance-authenticity-professionalism-5c

How do you balance professionalism and authenticity in an interview? (n.d). LinkedIn.

https://www.linkedin.com/advice/0/how-do-you-balance-professionalism-authenticity

How do you balance vulnerability and authenticity with professionalism and boundaries? (n.d). LinkedIn.

https://www.linkedin.com/advice/3/how-do-you-balance-vulnerability-authenticity-professionalism

How to tell if you're wearing a personality mask. (2020, September 1). Your Authentic Personality.

https://www.yourauthenticpersonality.com/how-to-tell-if-youre-wearing-a-personality-mask

Huong-Ha, T. (2021, March 16). 5 exercises to help you build more empathy. TED Conferences LLC.

https://ideas.ted.com/5-exercises-to-help-you-build-more-empathy

Igor. (2023, March 4). 75 inspiring reflection quotes on change, success, and life. Inspirationfeed.

https://inspirationfeed.com/reflection-quotes

Indeed Editorial Team. (2022, July 21). Empathic listening: Definition, examples and tips. Indeed.

https://www.indeed.com/career-advice/career-development/empathic-listening

Indeed Editorial Team. (2023, May 22). Active listening skills: A key to effective communication in the workplace. Indeed.

https://ca.indeed.com/career-advice/career-development/active-listening-skills

Jovanovic, J. (2023, March 23). Bringing more humanity, authenticity and intuition in the workplace. Is it possible?. LinkedIn.

https://www.linkedin.com/pulse/bringing-more-humanity-authenticity-intuition-jovana-jovanovic

Katz, L. (2021, May 24). How to develop authenticity in your relationships. Psychology Today.

https://www.psychologytoday.com/us/blog/here-we-are/202105/how-develop-authenticity-in-your-relationships

Learn to communicate authentically. (n.d). Government of Alberta.

https://alis.alberta.ca/succeed-at-work/make-your-work-life-more-satisfying/learn-to-communicate-authentically

Levoy, G. (2018, March 20). 37 questions to help you identify your passions. Psychology Today.

https://www.psychologytoday.com/us/blog/passion/201803/37-questions-help-you-identify-your-passions

Long, K. (2018, July 9). 6 steps to authentic communication. TheDailyPostive.

https://www.thedailypositive.com/6-steps-to-authentic-communication

Marie, S. (2022, April 18). 8 ways to build vulnerability in relationships. PsychCentral.

https://psychcentral.com/relationships/trust-and-vulnerability-in-relationships

Marshall, C. (2019, December 5). Authentic communication: The key to meaningful connection and engagement. Peak Grantmaking.

https://www.peakgrantmaking.org/insights/authentic-communication-the-key-to-meaningful-connection-and-engagement

Marty Rubin quote. (n.d). All Author. https://allauthor.com/quotes/280615

Maslow, A. H. (1943). A theory of human motivation. Psychological Review, 50(4), 370-396

Masterclass. (2022, August 1). What is masking? 3 examples of personality masking. Masterclass.

https://www.masterclass.com/articles/what-is-masking

Mcleod, S. (2023, June 14). Humanistic approach in psychology (Humanism): Definition and examples. Simply Psychology.

https://www.simplypsychology.org/humanistic

Merrill, M. S. (2004). Masks, metaphor and transformation: The communication of belief in ritual performance. Journal of Ritual Studies, 18(1), 16–33.

http://www.jstor.org/stable/44368668

Miller, K. (2020, March 13). How to increase self-awareness: 16 activities and tools. Positive Psychology.

https://positivepsychology.com/building-self-awareness-activities

Mind Tools Content Team. (n.d). Empathic listening. Mind Tools.

https://www.mindtools.com/a8l9j08/empathic-listening

Mind Tools Content Team. (2022). Active listening. Mind Tools.

https://www.mindtools.com/az4wxv7/active-listening

Morrill, Z. (2018, January 2). The importance of openness and authenticity in psychotherapy. Mad in America.

https://www.madinamerica.com/2018/01/importance-openness-authenticity-psychotherapy

Myles, S. (2013, July 22). Borderline personality disorder and the "Chameleon" effect. Sarah Myles.

https://sarahmyles.net/2013/07/22/borderline-personality-disorder-and-the-chameleon-effect

Ohwovoriole, T. (2021, April 28). What is the chameleon effect? Verywell Mind.

https://www.verywellmind.com/what-is-the-chameleon-effect-5114522

Oktar, K. & Lombrozo, T. (2022). Deciding to be authentic: Intuition is favored over deliberation when authenticity matters. Cognition, 223, 105021.

https://doi.org/10.1016/j.cognition.2022.105021

Oscar Wilde Quote: "Be yourself; everyone else is already taken." (n.d). QuoteFancy.

https://quotefancy.com/quote/14/Oscar-Wilde-Be-yourself-everyone-else-is-already-taken

Oyserman, D., Elmore, K., & Smith, G. C. (2012). Self, self-concept, and identity. In The Oxford Handbook of Human Motivation (pp. 1-36). Oxford University Press

Pace, R. (2021, August 11). How to develop authentic relationships. Marriage.com.

https://www.marriage.com/advice/relationship/how-to-develop-authentic-relationships

Pangilinan, J. (2023, March 28). 67 self-reflection quotes to help you grow as a person. Happier Human.

https://www.happierhuman.com/reflection-quotes

Petrilli, L. (2012, January 25). An introvert's guide to networking. Harvard Business Review.

https://hbr.org/2012/01/the-introverts-guide-to-networ

Pillay, H. (2014, March 23). Why it's important to know your strengths and weaknesses. Leaderonomics.com.

https://www.leaderonomics.com/articles/personal/why-its-important-to-know-your-strengths-and-weaknesses

The power of active listening: How to show empathy and understanding. (2017, July 25). Altura Learning.

https://www.alturalearning.com/the-power-of-active-listening-how-to-show-empathy-and-understanding

Psychology Today Staff. (2019a). Emotional intelligence. Psychology Today.

https://www.psychologytoday.com/us/basics/emotional-intelligence

Psychology Today Staff. (2019b). Identity. Psychology Today.

https://www.psychologytoday.com/us/basics/identity

Psychology Today Staff. (2019c). Perfectionism. Psychology Today.

https://www.psychologytoday.com/us/basics/perfectionism

Psychology Today Staff. (2020). Authenticity. Psychology Today.

https://www.psychologytoday.com/us/basics/authenticity

Ramya. (2021, March 5). 12 best ways to practice empathy and make it your real trait. Health Spectra.

https://www.healthspectra.com/best-ways-to-practice-empathy

Raypole, C. (2019, December 12). 10 tips for overcoming your fear of rejection. Healthline Media.

https://www.healthline.com/health/fear-of-rejection

Razzetti, G. (2018, March 8). How to be authentic in a fake world. Medium.

https://medium.com/personal-growth/being-authentic-in-a-fake-world-8458f240a227

Remove your mask now quote! (n.d). Pinterest.

https://www.pinterest.ca/pin/67061481926750559

Ridgeway, C. L., & Correll, S. J. (2004). Unpacking the gender system: A theoretical perspective on gender beliefs and social relations.

Gender & Society, 18(4), 510-531

Rosh, L. & Offermann, L. (2013, October). Be yourself, but carefully. Harvard Business Review.

https://hbr.org/2013/10/be-yourself-but-carefully

Sander, V. (2022, August 4). How to overcome your fear of being judged. SocialSelf.

https://socialself.com/blog/feeling-judged

Schmitz, T. (2016, June 3). The importance of emotional awareness in communication. Conover.

https://www.conovercompany.com/the-importance-of-emotional-awareness-in-communication

Schroll, A. (2017, June 14). 5 ways to overcome fear of judgment. HuffPost.

https://www.huffpost.com/entry/5-ways-to-overcome-fear-of-judgment_b_10396254

Scott, E. (2022, November 14). What is optimism? Verywell Mind.

https://www.verywellmind.com/the-benefits-of-optimism-3144811

Serwetz, R. (2022, June 15). Networking for introverts: 9 tips on how to meet new people. LifeHack.

https://www.lifehack.org/925730/networking-for-introverts

Sharma, S. (2023, February 24). 10 personality masks we wear to hide our true selves. Calm Sage.

https://www.calmsage.com/personality-masks-we-wear

Singh, A. (2021, July 19). How to stop your fear of being judged hold you back. CalmSage.

https://www.calmsage.com/how-to-stop-your-fear-of-being-judged

Small Business Team. (2020, September 25). How to practice empathy. SmallBusinessify.com.

https://smallbusinessify.com/how-to-practice-empathy

Spacey, A. (2017, May 12). The psychology of the mask and the real you. Hub Pages.

https://discover.hubpages.com/education/The-Gallery-of-the-Fool

Sparks, S. (2015, October 20). The masks that we wear. Psychology Today.

https://www.psychologytoday.com/us/blog/laugh-your-way-well-being/201510/the-masks-we-wear

Sutton, J. (2016, July 21). Active listening: The art of empathic conversation. Positive Psychology.

https://positivepsychology.com/active-listening/

Sutton, J. (2020, October 7). Understanding emotions: 15 ways to identify your feelings. Positive Psychology.

https://positivepsychology.com/understanding-emotions/

Sutton, J. (2021, September 24). What is perfectionism according to psychology? Positive Psychology.

https://positivepsychology.com/perfectionism/

Sweeney, M. (2022, June 17). How to network as an introvert. ZDNET.

https://www.zdnet.com/education/professional-development/how-to-network-as-an-introvert/

Tan, J. (2022). Hiding behind the "perfect" mask: a phenomenological study of Filipino university students' lived experiences of perfectionism, International Journal of Qualitative Studies on Health and Well-being, 17(1), DOI: 10.1080/17482631.2022.2062819

Tayloe, D. (2023, May 21). Why authenticity in relationships comes from these 12 habits. Power of Positivity.

https://www.powerofpositivity.com/authenticity-in-relationships/

Team Asana. (2021, November 29). 10 limiting beliefs and how to overcome them. Asana.

https://asana.com/resources/limiting-beliefs

TeamSoul. (2018, January 9). 5 keys to finding your authentic self and shedding your mask. Fearless Soul.

https://iamfearlesssoul.com/finding-your-authentic-self/

Thompson, M. (n.d). How to identify your strengths and weaknesses in 5 steps. LifeHack.

https://www.lifehack.org/887330/strengths-and-weaknesses

Tiodar, A. (2023, May 28). How to find your authentic self in a world of frauds. Subconscious Servant.

https://subconsciousservant.com/how-to-find-your-authentic-self/

Tiret, H. (2023, February 13). Active listening and empathy for human connection. Michigan State University.

https://www.canr.msu.edu/news/active-listening-and-empathy-for-human-connection

Tracey, B. (2017, October 19). How to overcome the fear of rejection. Brian Tracey International.

https://www.briantracy.com/blog/personal-success/fear-of-rejection/

Valdez, R. (2022, March 3). Understanding humanistic therapy. Verywell Health.

https://www.verywellhealth.com/humanistic-therapy-5216335

Varga, S. & Guignon, C. (2014, September 11). Authenticity. Stanford Encyclopedia of Philosophy.

https://plato.stanford.edu/entries/authenticity/

Walker, M. (2011, September 8). The five elements of adventure: Authenticity, purpose and inspiration. Psychology Today.

https://www.psychologytoday.com/us/blog/adventure-in-everything/201109/the-five-elements-adventure-authenticity-purpose-and-inspirati-0

Wanjohi, S. (2019, October 1). What I've learned from my self-awareness journey. The Book of Sarah.

https://thebookofsarah.com/what-ive-learned-from-my-self-awareness-journey

What is the martyr personality type? (2022, April 15). Know Your Archetypes.

https://knowyourarchetypes.com/martyr-personality-type/

Whitney-Coulter, A. (2021, February 5). Brene Brown on what it really means to trust. Mindful.

https://www.mindful.org/brene-brown-on-what-it-really-means-to-trust

Wikipedia Contributors. (2019a, March 23). Emotional intelligence. Wikipedia.

https://en.wikipedia.org/wiki/Emotional_intelligence

Wikipedia Contributors. (2019b, April 13). Nonverbal communication. Wikipedia.

https://en.wikipedia.org/wiki/Nonverbal_communication

Wikipedia Contributors. (2019c, May 9). Self-awareness. Wikipedia.

https://en.wikipedia.org/wiki/Self-awareness

Wikipedia Contributors. (2019d, May 23). Active listening. Wikipedia.

https://en.wikipedia.org/wiki/Active_listening

Williams, B. (2020, May 27). How to create self-acceptance and why you should. Forbes.

https://www.forbes.com/sites/theyec/2020/05/27/how-to-create-self-acceptance-and-why-you-should/?sh=5d7bc7f5154d

Willsey, P. (2021, August 24). Creating authentic connections. Psychology Today.

https://www.psychologytoday.com/us/blog/packing-success/202108/creating-authentic-connections

WomensMedia. (2021, October 2). 4 ways trusting your intuition is your superpower. Forbes.

https://www.forbes.com/sites/womensmedia/2021/10/02/4-ways-trusting-your-intuition-is-a-superpower/?sh=365d41f0c8e6

Wooll, M. (2022, July 19). Don't let limiting beliefs hold you back. Learn to overcome yours. BetterUp.

https://www.betterup.com/blog/what-are-limiting-beliefs

www.ingramcontent.com/pod-product-compliance
Lightning Source LLC
Chambersburg PA
CBHW071344080526
44587CB00017B/2961